UNDERCOVER

The Library of Espionage and Secret Warfare

The Smuggling Business

Timothy Green

CRESCENT BOOKS

Series Coordinator: John Mason
Picture Editor: Peter Cook
Designer: Ann Dunn
Editor: Mitzi Bales
Research: Elizabeth Lake
General Consultant: Beppie Harrison

Editorial Consultant:
ERIC CLARK

Crescent Books
A Division of Crown Publishers, Inc.

a b c d e f g h

ISBN 0-517-218690

Library of Congress Catalog
Card No. 76-56662

© 1977 Aldus Books Limited
First published in the United Kingdom
in 1977 by Aldus Books Limited

D. L.: S. S. 705/76

Printed and bound in Spain
by TONSA San Sebastian
and RONER Madrid

Drug addicts on city streets want the heroin they crave. Indians want the gold and watches they cannot buy in quantity. Italians want cheap cigarettes, and people in Europe and the United States want exotic pets. All these — and many more items — are illegally supplied the world over by smugglers. Today smuggling is big business run by powerful syndicates that operate internationally. This book, full of lively anecdotes and solid facts, tells how the smuggling trade is organized, what the smugglers provide, and who buys the illegal goods.

Contents

1 The Modern Smuggler   6

2 The Heroin Trail   22

3 Peddlers in Pot   44

4 The New Gold Rush   65

5 Undercover Diamonds   78

6 Trafficking in Treasure   94

7 Luxury Contraband   112

8 People, Parrots, and Pigs   126

Index   142

Picture Credits   144

Left: another exquisite work of art disappears from a church wall into the shadowy network of the art smugglers.

Frontispiece: a telephoto lens catches the deal that marks the end of the heroin trail.

The Modern Smuggler
1

There was no real reason to pay any special attention to the 1970 Dodge sedan that pulled up to the customs and immigration checkpoint on the United States side of the International Bridge over the Rio Grande in Laredo, Texas, late one evening. The driver was relaxed and all his documents were in order. Still, orders were orders, so the customs agent on duty routinely punched out the car's license number, TXF-57, on a computer terminal at his side, as he did for all vehicles crossing from Mexico. To his surprise the computer flashed back *hit*! Then the computer printed out added information: "TXF-57 used previously for suspected smuggling. Seen by informant parked near home of narc dealer, Monterrey, Mexico." The agent moved quickly to the car and asked the driver to step out.

A squad of customs agents immediately began to give the car a thorough going over. With high-powered lights they peered under the hood and fenders. They scanned the underside of the car with magnifying mirrors, took out the back seats, and prodded for hidden compartments. The search went on for more than two hours while the driver stood quietly by, seemingly unworried. Then, as one agent started to deflate the spare tire, he suddenly turned and sprinted across the bridge toward Mexico. An agent brought him down with a flying tackle and took him back. When the tire was cut open, 11 kilograms (more than 24 pounds) of pure heroin was found inside. When cut and repackaged, these 11 kilos would be worth $2.5 million on the American street market. The vital tip-off from the computer, which was primed with all the latest intelligence gossip, prevented it from getting there.

Today, customs officials combating the gigantic web of modern smuggling need every aid that technology can place at their hands, because the jet age has made the smuggler one of the most mobile men on earth. He is the complete international man. Armed with a fistful of passports he can change his identity like a chameleon, and in a matter of hours flit thousands of miles across half a dozen frontiers. Take Hans Anderegg, for instance. He was a gold smuggler traveling under the guise of a salesman for a Swiss duplicating firm. When he was arrested with $36,000 in gold in a specially made jacket beneath his shirt, he

Right: a smuggler loads his specially designed vest with gold bars. Gold is one of the many commodities that is marketed illegally the world over. The desire for gold never appears to abate—and smuggling rings big and small never seem short of the desired product.

Above: 18th-century engraving of smugglers coming ashore. Wherever there have been duties or tariffs—or prohibited imports—there have always been smugglers to provide the goods.

had in his pocket an airline ticket routing him from Geneva to Bangkok by way of Frankfurt, Nicosia, Istanbul, Beirut, Vancouver, Tokyo, Hong Kong, Manila, and Jakarta. Another gold smuggler, arrested at John F. Kennedy Airport in New York, had tickets taking him from Zurich to Rio de Janeiro, Caracas, Mexico City, New York, and finally back to Zurich.

The smuggler in many ways is just another international businessman—and his turnover would do credit to many international corporations. His business happens to be illegal and risky, but look at the stakes involved: $5 billion worth of heroin smuggled into the United States each year, and $1.5 billion in gold passing annually along smuggling pipelines to India and Indonesia, to France and Morocco, to Brazil and Turkey. Perhaps half of all the watches made in Switzerland reach their eventual wearers by some back door. At least a quarter of all the diamonds found in Sierra Leone are smuggled out of the country by illegal diggers. Stolen art treasures from Italy and France cross the Atlantic into private collections in North and South America or go east to the oil sheikdoms. Precious relics of antiquity are spirited from Greece, Turkey, Iran, Egypt, and Mexico into the display cases of American museums whose directors' ethics are often overwhelmed by zeal.

The modern smuggler, in fact, is in business to provide whatever his client requires, be it diamonds or contraband parrots— which, incidentally, are made drunk to keep them quiet in transit. There are even flourishing lines in smuggling food; fine beefsteaks, for example, are smuggled from France into Italy to get around Common Market price regulations. Nearly one-

Left: the crew of a dhow leaving Dubai on the Persian Gulf for the 10-day trip to the west coast of India, with a cargo of smuggled gold.

Below: not all smugglers get away with it. The amateur is often the most vulnerable, and Mike Harris, a young American, was sentenced to six years in a Spanish jail for attempting to bring marijuana into Spain— one of hundreds of Americans in foreign prisons for taking part in the drugs traffic.

third of Ghana's cocoa crop is smuggled out through neighboring Togo and the Ivory Coast to enable the growers to obtain hard money—dollars or pounds sterling—paid into accounts abroad. Most of this illicit trade is carried on with all the efficiency of any multinational company. Entirely legitimate businesses, such as a travel bureau or an import-export agency, are also often fronts for smuggling organizations. One of the world's largest gold smugglers also owned and operated the franchise for a leading make of British car in a small Middle Eastern country. He made a good profit from both activities.

A smuggling syndicate operates much like any other business. The boss is really a chief executive. He makes all the plans, establishes international contacts, and thinks up the smuggling routes and method—but remains aloof from actual operations. He is aided by a handful of managers looking after such specialties as financing, travel (one reason why many smuggling syndicates find it handy to have their own travel agency), the bribing of airline or customs officials, and the recruitment of couriers, or "mules" as they are called. There may also be someone in charge of local arrangements in the countries to which the smuggled goods is going.

There is still another similarity between legitimate business and its illegal counterpart: price fluctuation. Just as the prices of products traded legally vary with quality and market conditions such as supply and demand, so do the prices of goods go up and down in the smuggling trade. Consider the price of drugs. Heroin and cannabis, in whatever form or by whatever name, come in several grades, each with a going price. Of course, the wholesale price at which big dealers sell to big dealers is less than the street price. When the authorities are successful in reducing the supply by seizures, the price of all grades rises. The greater the heat, the steeper the price.

Supply and Demand

The price of such smuggled goods as gold, diamonds, and watches closely reflects the fluctuations in the legitimate markets of New York, London, Antwerp, and Zurich.

Because the events in this book cover a period of several years from the late 1960s to the mid-1970s, the value put upon smuggled items will differ. Prices are what they were at the time of the case described.

The headquarters of a smuggling syndicate will usually be in one of a handful of cities that are strategically close to other countries with much tighter import restrictions. Cities such as Geneva and Brussels in Europe, Beirut and Dubai in the Middle East, Singapore and Hong Kong in Asia, and Tijuana in Mexico make ideal launching pads. On their home ground the smugglers—except those dealing in narcotics—are usually not in violation of local laws, and carry on their activities undisturbed.

The challenge of constantly trying to outwit the authorities can be stimulating, and smuggling can become a passion, like gambling. Many people, once in it, never really quit. One family that worked for years smuggling gold out of Beirut into Iran and Japan later emigrated to a South American republic. Within a short time of arriving in their new homeland they were back in harness smuggling gold in a big way. "You don't feel happy unless you have a line open and someone making a run for you," one of them declared.

Although the top men obviously must work together, most of a syndicate's small fry, especially the mules, know only their immediate contacts. If caught there is little they can give away.

A mule probably will not even know the name of the person who gives him his instructions, nor how to get in touch with him. Usually he doesn't know the person to whom he has to make delivery. He will be told just to sit tight in a certain hotel or bar until someone contacts him. In this way if he is *blown*— that is, recognized but not necessarily arrested—coming through airport customs he cannot unwittingly lead agents to the next link in the chain. All the person at the receiving end has to do is hang around the airport among the waiting crowd, and see that the mule comes through safely. If he does not, he is simply written off as a loss. To make identification of mules easier, several syndicates have devised their own "club ties" so that a mule wearing one can immediately be picked out.

Mules often receive careful training before embarking on their first journey. One Beirut organization, for example, uses a room with three airline seats in it. There the trainee mules sit for hours on end wearing weighted smuggling vests beneath their clothes, so that they become accustomed to standing up after a long flight in a natural way, and without revealing what they are carrying. An outfit in Brussels maintained a comfortable apartment where the mules could relax and get a firm grip on themselves on the night before their first journey; they were helped to dress before setting out for the airport in the morning. More often than not a courier will not know precisely where he is going or what his flight number is until he is actually handed his tickets at the airport. This prevents the careless boast in some bar or to a girl friend the night before, "I'm off to Rio in the morning on a little smuggling job."

Mules occasionally run off with the goods to keep the profit themselves. As insurance against this, a syndicate often sends a high-up on the same plane to keep a wary eye on couriers, particularly new ones. Even then, things can go badly wrong. One international currency smuggler who was having trouble getting money out of Britain was offered help by a group of men who said they were in a position to "fix things"—for a fee, of course. Foolishly, the smuggler agreed to accept their help. When he got to London's Heathrow Airport, he handed over to one of the men a black suitcase containing nearly $90,000 in cash, destined for Frankfurt. Just to keep an eye on things, the smuggler went along on the same plane. When they landed at Frankfurt he was handed back his suitcase. He beat a straight path to the men's toilet, opened the case, and found only old clothes. The courier had switched suitcases en route, but the smuggler could hardly run to the police and complain that "the man who was smuggling money out of England for me has stolen it."

Smuggling syndicates always have to be careful not to hire known criminals as mules, partly to make sure the shipments are not stolen, but more so because a man or woman with a record may be on the undesirable alien lists maintained at many airport immigration desks, and may be turned back. The preferred mules are students, taxi drivers, or salespeople from

Below: Salvador Pardo-Bolland (left), was the Mexican ambassador to Bolivia in 1964 when he was arrested by police in New York and accused of smuggling 50 kilos of heroin from France. Right: two of the suitcases used by Pardo-Bolland, which police discovered were filled with heroin. The ambassador had checked them in baggage lockers during a stopover in Montreal, and the Canadian police, tipped off by agents in France, opened them.

department stores and boutiques. They are easy to contact and are often willing to make an occasional trip for a thrill and some extra tax-free pocket money. One young German couple from Munich got a free honeymoon by carrying gold on the way out.

Mules that Fly

Airline crews make ideal mules. They travel constantly and usually pass through customs controls with minimum or no fuss. Over the years almost every international airline has had trouble with smugglers among its staff. Corsican smugglers sending heroin to the United States once corrupted an Air France dispatcher, who gave them some say in assigning crews for particular flights. When they had a shipment of heroin to go to the States, the smugglers could arrange for a steward in their employ to be put on a New York-bound flight.

The Corsicans were even able to use the Air France telex network for sending coded delivery instructions to the steward when he arrived at the other end. He would be told that a room had been reserved for him at a certain hotel. All he had to do then was go there and wait to be contacted. If a message said that the hotel in which he had expected to stay was full, it meant that something had gone wrong, and he should wait for further instructions.

A diplomatic passport is another perfect front for smuggling because a member of a diplomatic corps is usually immune from casual customs searches. Because of this, many diplomats,

especially from small South American and African countries, have become globe-trotting smugglers carrying everything from diamonds to heroin in their diplomatic bags. So many diplomats are mules that the joke in smuggling circles is that the letters C.D., which stand for *Corps Diplomatique*, should really mean *Contrabandier Distingué*, or distinguished smuggler.

In the late 1960s the Guatamalan Ambassador to the Netherlands and Belgium always made a habit of stopping over in New York for a few days on his way back home from Europe. Because he was on official business, or said he was, his baggage was not searched when he came into New York. But after a tip-off the customs began to look into his travel habits. They noted that his checked baggage was often much heavier when he arrived than when he left. Was he leaving large presents with a mistress? Diplomatic immunity is not entirely sacrosanct; it was time to have a look. One day the ambassador was stopped by narcotics agents just as he was getting into a cab outside his hotel. He had with him a suitcase containing 50 kilos of heroin and $26,000 in cash. The money, he confessed later, was his fee for each delivery.

No sooner was the ambassador in jail than the narcotics agents got a whisper from an informant, "Well, you got one of them, but you haven't got the other." Finding the "other"

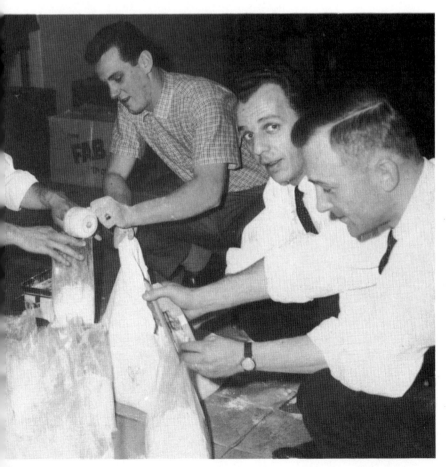

Left: police substituting flour for all but two kilos of Pardo-Bolland's heroin in Montreal. The next day the unsuspecting diplomat picked up his bags and flew to New York—and arrest.

took three years. Agents on both sides of the Atlantic sifted through stacks of airline passenger manifests and overseas cables. They picked up some reference to a courier known as "Lambo." This name could a be a shortened form of *L'ambassador*, but which ambassador? Over the months they noted some pattern emerging. The visits to New York of Gilbert Coscia, a suspected Corsican narcotics trafficker, coincided with remarkable consistency with the travels of the Mexican Ambassador to Bolivia, Salvador Pardo-Bolland. The evidence was purely circumstantial, however—not nearly good enough for an arrest of a diplomat. He was put under surveillance. One day he showed up in Nice, France, where, in the company of Juan Aritzi, an Uruguayan diplomat, he was observed by undercover agents talking with Coscia. A day or two later Pardo-Bolland took off for New York while his Uruguayan friend flew to Montreal with six suitcases. Upon disembarking, Aritzi waved his

Above: Teresa Laws (left) and Lynn Francis, two young English girls who discovered that the presents their Kenyan host had asked them to take to London were illegal packages of traveler's checks and currency. The girls were held in Kenya for two months awaiting trial, but in the end were sent back to their homes in England.

Right: Chief Superintendent Toorenaan of the Amsterdam police with a selection of interesting items in which drugs were discovered. In any form of smuggling, ingenuity is the smuggler's best friend.

diplomatic passport, and he and his six bags went through Canadian customs without search. But while the South American diplomat had been high over the Atlantic enjoying his champagne in the first class cabin, messages had flashed from the United States agents in France to the Mounties in Canada.

Undercover mounties, who had been waiting in the arrival hall crowd, followed the unsuspecting diplomat as he left four of the suitcases in the baggage lockers at Montreal Central Railroad Station, and checked himself into a nearby hotel. While he slept, the mounties opened the lockers and examined the suitcases. They found 50 kilos of heroin, done up neatly in one kilo bags. It was worth $12 million at street prices in any North American city. The mounties substituted flour for all but two kilos of heroin, and put the cases back in the lockers. Next morning the diplomat reclaimed his bags, set off for New York, and checked into the Elysee Hotel where Ambassador Pardo-Bolland was waiting for him. A couple of days later they made their delivery to a French contact staying at the Americana Hotel—and hurried off to book themselves on the next flight to South America. Narcotics men grabbed them at the airport and arrested the French contact at the hotel.

The Unwitting Mules

The smuggler, of course, is always seeking out mules who will attract the least attention as they go through customs. In recent years they have even resorted to children. Take the case of the two young English schoolgirls, Teresa L., 14, and Lynn F., 16. They were offered a 10-day holiday in Kenya by a kindly Indian woman in whose south London grocery store Teresa worked on weekends. When they landed in Nairobi, the two girls were looked after by the woman's equally kind and gracious husband, who made their vacation enjoyable with sightseeing and visits to game parks. When they were about to leave to return to London, their host asked them to take some packages which, he said, were presents for his wife and other friends in England. At Nairobi airport, just before the girls boarded the plane, their baggage was searched. Concealed within a copper lampstand and two handbags that the girls were taking back as gifts was the equivalent of $240,000 in traveler's checks and currency. The two girls had no idea that it was there or that they were being used to smuggle currency out of Kenya and into Britain. The smugglers had counted on the customs officials paying little attention to a couple of schoolgirls, but the authorities had been tipped off. Although the girls were caught, their Kenyan host was already safely en route to Switzerland when the hue and cry was raised. The two teenagers spent a miserable two months awaiting trial, but were then discharged.

Old people also have often been enticed into acting as mules, because the smugglers feel they will attract little attention. An American heroin dealer offered two California grandmothers

Above: a miniature submarine captured at Lake Maggiore on the Italian-Swiss border. The Italian government has a monopoly on cigarette sales, and foreign cigarettes cost about five times as much as they do over the border in Switzerland. This difference provides the basis of a thriving trade in contraband cigarettes. This sub was an ingenious method to get the cigarettes across the Lake; it works by means of pedals.

bonuses big enough to enable them to enjoy a comfortable old age if they would bring in heroin from Mexico City. Instead they ended up in the misery of a Mexican prison.

Mules will naturally try all kinds of tricks to frustrate the customs. A young man from San Francisco tried hiding cocaine in a plaster leg cast, but was picked up because a Mexican customs official noticed he was having difficulty remembering which leg to favor; he had overlooked the necessity of practicing his limp. A pretty young Hollywood girl taped packets of cocaine across her lower abdomen in a fairly common ploy to look pregnant. She lacked that rather stately and serene walk of the truly pregnant woman, however, and the customs official's sharp eyes singled her out.

The ingenuity of the smuggler's mind is virtually limitless. A crate of six hissing boa constrictors arrived at Miami Airport one day addressed to a local zoo. A nervous customs agent,

Above: as the smugglers are by definition international, so must the law forces have some system of international cooperation to combat them. This team of narcotic agents in Istanbul, Turkey, at the start of one heroin trail, work with police around the world to stop the deadly but profitable traffic in Turkish opium.

poking about inside with a stick, found that the snakes were reclining happily on a bed of marijuana leaves. A Donald Duck statue coming into New York from Antwerp had $250,000 worth of cut and polished diamonds concealed in a secret compartment. One businessman's "aftershave lotion" was enough LSD for 100,000 trips.

The sheer volume of international sea and air freight today makes it impossible for the authorities to check every crate individually. Much smuggling can therefore be carried out simply by false customs declarations and other forms of creative paperwork. A consignment of "agricultural machine spares" will really hide a consignment of gold, or a crate of "television tubes"

Right: a United States customs
agent on a stake-out in a bar
just over the Mexican border,
one of a small army of men
working to stop the drug
smugglers operating over the
Mexico-United States border.

Below: sophisticated equipment
in use by the Narcotics Service
in Marseilles, an important stop
on the heroin route from Turkey.

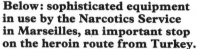

will conceal a thousand Swiss watches. British customs officers
once found 80 kilos of marijuana carefully hidden in a consignment of mango pickles that arrived at the London docks from
Pakistan. Nine cans in a total shipment of 410 had been opened
up, the pickles taken out, and cannabis put in. A thin layer of
pickles had then been spread on top, and the tins resealed.

Smuggling by Bookkeeping

Increasingly, smuggling involves not only such forbidden
goods as narcotics, gold, and other high-duty items such as
watches and precious stones, but also ordinary goods as varied
as Christmas tree decorations or shoes, all of them legal. For
smuggling of this type, the elaborate ruses of fake casts, false
pregnancies, or canned marijuana, are not necessary. Creative
bookkeeping does the job. The goods are imported openly, but
the declaration of the value or the number of articles is false. This
action technically is smuggling, and has grown up with higher
import duties and taxes. A New York shoe importer bringing in,
say, 50,000 pairs of shoes from Italy, declares only 40,000 on the
documents on the fairly safe gamble that no customs officer has
time to count the shipment. The importer then has 10,000 pairs
of duty-free shoes to sell. They do not appear on his books, and
can be disposed of without declaring the profits to the taxman.

Unmasking the endless variety of tricks is usually not a matter
of chance or sudden insight. Rather, it requires many weeks,
even months, of painstaking investigation. Today, most customs
activity is devoted not to catching the occasional traveler with a
bottle of Scotch more than his duty-free allowance, or even the
lady with an undeclared mink, but to controlling professional
organized smuggling. The amateur will eventually be caught
anyway, most often because he gives himself away by nervous-
ness or overconfidence. He may be foolish enough to select the
inspector with the longest line on the mistaken theory that by

the time it is his turn the officer will whisk him through to speed up the backlog. The amateur who is arrested is purely a bonus.

To match the massive growth of smuggling in recent years, customs and police forces have often been completely reorganized to tackle the increasing efficiency of professionals, and to cope with their quick adaptation of every technical development to their businesslike crime. In an attempt to end a long standing rivalry between two organizations that sometimes got in the way of solving cases, the United States Bureau of Narcotics and Dangerous Drugs and the drugs squad of the United States Customs Agency Service, the detective division of customs, were merged in 1973 into the Drug Enforcement Agency. The United States Bureau of Customs now maintains its own experts in everything from diamonds to Swiss watches. It even has 12 laboratories whose technicians can determine whether French perfume declared as being a cheap brand worth $5 a bottle is just that, or really some exotic version that costs 20 times as much.

In Europe, the Italians have set up a special squad to concentrate on recovering stolen and smuggled works of art. Scotland Yard also has a special Art and Antiques Squad, while the flood of illegal Asian immigrants smuggled into Britain has prompted

Right: a police photograph of 1926 shows New York port police searching a Chinese seaman suspected of opium smuggling. Modern customs forces have advanced far beyond the old-fashioned body search in techniques to catch smugglers.

the Yard to create an Illegal Immigration Unit dedicated purely to catching the smugglers of people.

The inspectors who scrutinize the ordinary traveler coming off a plane or cruise ship are merely the uniformed front men. Working behind the scenes—frequently undercover—is a small army of customs detectives. Their job is to ferret out who is really behind the rackets, and to get the hard evidence to prove it in court. "It is rather like trying to unravel a plate of spaghetti," said a customs agent. "You think one strand is the key to the whole thing, but it leads you nowhere. Even when you have arrested a smuggler you are sure is important, someone else pops up in his place a few months later."

Modern technology is a vital ally. In 1971 the United States Bureau of Customs first installed ADPRIN—Automated Data Processing Intelligence Network—at most ports of entry so that an agent could check instantly to see if anything suspicious was known of any incoming person, vehicle, or ship. It triggered off 686 productive hits and 444 arrests in the first year—including the heroin smuggler tackled on the bridge in Laredo. Sophisticated x-ray machines, devised to beat hijackers, are also invaluable for catching goods smuggled in baggage or freight. Nevertheless, in the end there is no substitute for good old-fashioned leg work and, above all, developing underworld contacts who can give tip-offs. "The best scientific aid I know," remarked a customs agent, "is a good informer."

Even an obscure tip-off may yield surprising results. An American undercover narcotics agent investigating heroin smuggling from Marseilles once got a tip that a garage in the French seaport was being used to make special compartments in

Above left: x-ray machines developed to screen luggage for concealed arms as part of airport anti-hijack procedures have an equally important role in detecting other prohibited articles being smuggled out.

Above: a border terminal—this one at Laredo, Texas— of the Treasury Enforcement Communications System, which can check license plates of vehicles entering the United States against a vast computer bank of suspicious cars and trucks.

Citroën cars and 1971-model Volkswagen campers. That was not much to go on, but the word was fed back into the computerized intelligence network and stored there. Some months later a Volkswagon camper was being offloaded from a ship at Elizabeth, New Jersey. A routine computer check by a local customs agent alerted him to the fact that such vehicles should be scrutinized carefully. Sure enough, beneath the floor and in the water tank he came upon 45 kilos of heroin, worth millions of dollars, all neatly packaged in polythene bags.

Much of the time the undercover agents' task is like a game of cat and mouse. He may be fairly sure who the ringleaders of a group are, and they know he knows. But he lacks the vital evidence to prove it. "I often go out to dinner with a smuggler here," said an American undercover agent in Hong Kong, "and we have a fine time. What I'm really hoping is that after a few drinks he'll let slip something about some other operator. One smuggler may be disgruntled with another, so he'll help me." The professional smugglers are only too ready to tip off agents to any amateur or newcomer who tries to muscle in on their preserve. They will usually let the nonprofessional get away with two or three small shipments until, with his confidence bolstered, he tries a larger consignment. Then a simple phone call makes sure that either he or his mule is caught—sometimes both.

The handicap for many customs services is that they are frequently limited to investigations within their own frontiers, while the smugglers themselves roam free. Customs men can liaise with colleagues abroad through Interpol, but they can rarely match the smugglers' disregard for frontiers. Only the

Left: behind all the new and sophisticated technology, the smuggler and the lawman still operate the old cat-and-mouse game. Here customs agents in Laredo, Texas, wait in a motel room on a stake-out, watching for a narcotics smuggler.

Right: an Italian customs agent captures a cigarette smuggler creeping through the rough country on the Italian-Swiss border. In general, customs officials figure that only 10 percent of all smugglers are ever caught. This officer at least knows that there is now one cigarette smuggler less.

Americans maintain agents stationed permanently abroad. Both the Bureau of Customs and the Drug Enforcement Agency have active agents around the world. The DEA, in fact, spends much of its $250 million annual budget overseas, operating a network of undercover agents throughout France, Turkey, the Middle East, Southeast Asia, and South America on the trail of heroin and cocaine. Except in the United States, they lack powers of arrest, and must always work closely with local police or customs services. Often they do all the hard and even dangerous under-cover work, and then present the finished case to the local police who move in to make the arrest—and get the glory. "My job is to show them where to go, and then to run," said an American agent in France, slightly bitterly, "so that I am not around when the actual arrest is made."

Undercover agents are often so effective that when they finally reveal themselves their quarry is aghast. One British customs agent worked for months in London and Pakistan to track down a gang of cannabis smugglers. He found that the cannabis was coming into England by ship in falsely labeled containers. He finally succeeded in intercepting a consignment at the docks, and substituting gravel for the cannabis. He then went along on the delivery truck to hand over the crates to an import-export firm in the London suburbs. Under the watchful eyes of the chief smuggler, whom he had been tracking for months, the customs man helped the truck driver unload and stack the crates. The pleased smuggler gave him a tip. The customs agent declined the gratuity and then revealed his true identity. The smuggler thought he was joking—until he slipped on the handcuffs.

Right: the opium poppy harvest in Turkey. Opium is grown legally and sold to the government opium-buying monopoly, which exports it for use in making medicines. But many farmers grow more than they declare and sell the excess to the black market—and it is then on the opium trail that leads to heroin-hungry addicts around the world, doubling and redoubling its price until it is sold on the streets at about 1000 times the farmer's price. Below: the addict and his fix.

The Heroin Trail

2

The two light planes high over southern Florida seemed to be playing a subtle game of follow-the-leader in the bright morning air. The pace was set by the single-engined Cessna 210 that ducked and dodged from the shelter of one cloud to another. At its controls was Cesar Medice Bianchi, a chunky, black-haired man who kept glancing nervously at the skies over his shoulder as he desperately tried to figure out what the unmarked Skymaster tailing him through the clouds was up to.

The Skymaster had taken off from Miami International Airport moments after he had, and was now clinging to his tail like a cat after a mouse. Had his little game been rumbled? There had been no sign of any trouble when he had touched down at Miami the previous evening after a grueling five-day flight of almost 4000 miles. He had flown the 210 from a private landing strip in Paraguay over the Andes, up the west coast of South America to

Panama, and then across the Caribbean to the shores of Florida. He had been paid no special attention as he and his copilot Renato Balestra had checked through customs and gone to a hotel to rest. But this morning, back in the air, there was that damned Skymaster forever on his tail.

Bianchi's official flight plan, filed with the Civil Aeronautics Authority, said he was going to St. Petersburg, but he was really headed for another airport in North Perry where he had parked his car two weeks ago before taking off for Paraguay. Should he go there or to St. Petersburg? The trouble was he couldn't discuss it with Balestra. The young copilot knew about the false flight plan, but he didn't know that tucked in behind the auxiliary fuel tank were three carryall bags crammed with 43 kilos of almost pure white heroin. This illicit cargo was worth over $10 million on the streets of America. Balestra knew that Bianchi was a regular smuggler—a *contrabandista*—of cigarettes, whisky, and other luxury items from the United States into South America, but not that his friend had taken to hauling narcotics on the way back.

So, not wanting to get Balestra's wind up by drawing attention to the plane on their tail, Bianchi decided to follow their original scheme to fly into North Perry. On the ground he made no attempt to offload the heroin, especially when he saw the Skymaster land too. Instead he headed for his car, and drove back into Miami to hole up in a hotel. Next morning he went to his bank, drew out his total savings of $26,000, and, leaving Balestra to fend for himself, drove to the airport to buy a ticket on the next jet bound for the comparative safety of South America. He never made it. United States customs men stepped in and arrested him, just as they had Balestra.

Bianchi had been right to worry. The men in the Skymaster had been customs agents hard on his trail from the moment he arrived in the United States. During the night they had searched his plane and found his illegal cargo—one of the biggest drug hauls in the long-running, bitter war between American narcotic agents and the drug smugglers.

Bianchi, of course, was small fry, a little link in the chain that leads all the way from the opium fields of Afyon (which means opium) Province in Turkey to the streets of New York, Chicago, Detroit, and a score of other large American cities where most of America's 500,000 heroin addicts slowly destroy themselves.

Above: the $1 million cargo of heroin that was flown from Paraguay to the United States by smuggler Cesar Medice Bianchi at the time that he was caught and arrested in Miami. The heroin haul was fancifully packaged like gift parcels in colorful Christmas wrappings.

Who Was Bianchi's Boss?

The taking of Bianchi was, however, a vital breakthrough for the narcotics agents. It proved that they were dealing not just with a "French Connection," but also with a Latin American Connection that was equally dangerous. The facts of the case, peeled away layer by layer, unveiled an organization controlled through Paraguay. It had moved some 5000 kilos of heroin, worth almost $2 billion, into the United States over a period of years. The trail led right to Auguste Joseph Ricord—variously known as "Monsieur Andre" and "El Commandante"—an expatriate Corsican who ran the Paris-Nice Motel just outside the Paraguayan capital of Asunción.

At that moment in time, however, the Miami-based agents knew nothing of El Commandante, the mastermind behind the Latin American Connection. They simply had the pilot Bianchi, his plane, and a large haul of pure heroin. Bianchi and Balestra had been caught because of a tip-off from a disgruntled fellow contrabandista. The agents wanted to capitalize on his seizure, but how? Could he be persuaded to cooperate and go on as if nothing had happened in order to lead the agents to the rest of the gang? This is what narcotics or customs agents try with most couriers they catch. A conviction for smuggling narcotics

into the United States may lead to 20 years in jail, but a man who helps the authorities may get away with five. So there is plenty of incentive to play ball. But any decision by the arrested smuggler must be quick. He cannot be out of circulation too long, and he has to go through the motions of making any expected delivery.

The pressures on Cesar Bianchi to cooperate were intense. He had a wife and family in Argentina, and the agents told him bluntly that if he did not help he would be an old man before he saw them again. So he admitted that he had already sent a cable saying he had arrived safely, and that he had been instructed to keep phoning the Four Ambassadors Hotel in Miami until a contact man arrived. The game then began.

For the next seven days the net was cast. Bianchi went to the hotel and made contact with a Paraguayan, Felix Becker, and an Argentine, Aron Muravnik. Becker told him to drive the heroin to New York, check into a motel, and await further instructions. The customs men now had to watch not only Bianchi, but also Becker and Muravnik around the clock, knowing that if they gave themselves away for a second the whole plan would be blown. They had to have the evidence of actual delivery of the heroin to make a case stand up.

As they trailed Becker and Muravnik along the streets and through the bars of New York, other members of the gang surfaced. In the Hilton Hotel the South Americans linked up with Pierre Gahou, a Frenchman, who was making final arrangements with the buyer. He kept meeting a young man with a lissome blonde girl friend in a blue Volkswagen. The customs men could not immediately identify the young man, but he seemed to be the man with the money. They never had a chance to find out. On the crucial night that the actual delivery was to be made Becker and Bianchi drove through Manhattan with the heroin. Becker, realizing they were being followed, tried to jump out of the car—and found himself looking down the barrel of a narcotics agent's gun. Now there was no hope of completing the delivery, so the rest of the known dope smugglers were swiftly rounded up.

Five men were in the bag: Bianchi, his copilot Balestra, Becker, Muravnik, and Gahou. But that was rather like nipping off one tentacle of an octopus. The other tentacles are an equal threat unless the body itself is destroyed—and the body was Auguste Ricord, sitting safely in the Paris-Nice Motel, 5000 miles away in Paraguay.

In the following months of grueling cross-examination of the five arrested men, a clearer picture of Ricord's organization began to emerge. The Bianchi case, the customs men soon realized, fitted in neatly with a number of other seizures of heroin coming from South America. For instance, there had been the case in which no less than 13 out-of-work Argentines and Brazilians had been picked up coming into the United States, each with about five kilos of heroin in false bottomed

Below: Auguste Ricord, the top man in the Latin American Connection that brought in many thousands of kilos of heroin to the desperate addicts who live in the United States. It took almost two years—and intense political pressure— to extradite Ricord from Paraguay.

suitcases or taped to their bodies. Each had a tourist visa issued by the United States Embassy in Buenos Aires. And Auguste Ricord just happened to have lived in Buenos Aires for a while. Another seizure had been made of heroin hidden in plastic bags at the bottom of bottles of choice Chilean red wine brought in by travelers as part of their duty-free allowance from South America. The Bianchi case indicated that now, instead of sending in perhaps 10 or 20 mules each with a few kilos, the Latin American syndicate was making large single shipments by air.

A careful study of the air routes to and from South America used by the *contrabandista* planes revealed that they all went through Panama's Tecumen Airport. It was the pivot point in the whole operation. Agents from the Bureau of Narcotics and Dangerous Drugs were able to establish that one man controlled the permissions to fly in and out of the airport. That was the Chief of Air Traffic Control, Joaquim Him. The next step was to recruit a former convict who was willing to infiltrate one of the smuggling groups operating through Panama with Him's blessing.

One steamy night in Panama, the undercover agent was on hand as Him presided over the transfer of a suitcase full of cocaine to be flown into Texas. Another undercover agent, posing as a buyer for the Mafia, was also in the room. The vital evidence was now available, but Him was untouchable in Panama. The agents knew, however, that Him was an avid softball player and manager of the Tecumen Airport team. From time to time he took the Tecumen ball players into the United States-controlled Panama Canal Zone for a game against the Americans. A few

days later as Him drove happily into the Zone, probably thinking about his batting order, his car was surrounded by narcotic agents. "You are on United States territory; you are under arrest," he was told. A waiting plane whisked him back to the United States for trial.

The arrest of Joaquim Him lopped off a big tentacle of the narcotics octopus. It also served as a trial run for getting to El Commandante himself in Paraguay. Clearly the United States agents could not kidnap him and spirit him out of the country covertly. Any attempt to snatch El Commandante on Paraguay's sovereign territory would lead to diplomatic repercussions. Besides, if Ricord was to be taken outside the law, the case against him might be thrown out of court. Clearly he had to be arrested and extradited formally.

Six months after the arrest of Bianchi, and three months after the arrest of Him in Panama, the Americans felt confident that they had sufficient hard evidence to charge Ricord with conspiracy to smuggle heroin into the United States. A formal request went through the United States Embassy to the Paraguayan government asking the police to arrest and hold him.

One afternoon a few days later a police car drew up outside the Paris-Nice Motel in Asunción, and a young policeman went inside and asked for Ricord. A short elderly man told the officer he did not know where Ricord was. He might be in the office, the man said, and directed the cop there. As the policeman went off on his search, the elderly man—now moving with a speed that belied his age—hurried out of the motel with a briefcase, jumped into his car, and took off at high speed for the ferry to Argentina. The cop, realizing he had been fooled, set off in hot pursuit and caught up with the fleeing racketeer before he could get on the boat. Ricord offered no resistance.

It took almost two years from the time of arrest before Ricord was brought to the United States for trial. For months he lived comfortably in Asunción prison, where he received visitors and dined on good French cooking brought in from his own restaurant. Many people felt he was still running the operation from his cell. But having got him cornered, the Americans would not let go. Finally, after President Nixon had threatened that the United States would cut off all lines of credit to Paraguay, and a personal emissary from Nixon had called on Paraguay's president, the Paraguayans gave way. Ricord was flown to New York, tried, and sentenced to 20 years in jail—the first time this ever happened to a person who had never committed a crime in the United States or even set foot on American soil before his trial. Bianchi and Balestra had their sentences reduced because they testified against Ricord.

With Ricord in prison, his whole syndicate collapsed. The Latin American Connection was broken.

The case of Auguste Ricord is something of a classic in the annals of narcotics smuggling because a whole syndicate was brought down. Too often only individual arms are lopped off,

27

The Worldwide Connection

This spider's web of drug routes links the chief opium producing areas of Turkey and Southeast Asia with the main consumer, the United States. For years the key link-up was the French Connection, so called because the opium from Turkey was first filtered to France to be made up into heroin, and from there spirited to the United States.

At first the route was direct from Marseilles or Paris to New York, but gradually the smugglers had to become more devious to outwit the narcotics agents. They diversified, sending consignments via Montreal, Mexico City, Panama, or Paraguay.

American involvement in the Vietnam war gave a new impetus to the drug traffic from Southeast Asia. Previously the drugs grown in the Shan States of Burma had been chiefly used by the orient's addicts in such cities as Bangkok, Singapore, and Hong Kong. But unscrupulous people, seeing the profits to be made, started dispatching heroin across the Pacific. The initial route was via Australia, but that was quickly detected, and the main supply routes in recent years have been from Bangkok, Singapore, Penang, or Hong Kong. The biggest traffic is between Bangkok and Hong Kong, in which American drug dealers feel most at ease in a largely English-speaking community.

The map shows the known routes. From the smugglers' point of view, their greatest successes are the routes not shown—for the simple reason that they remain undetected.

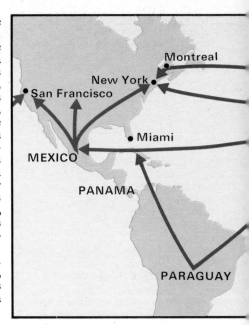

while the main organization continues. The case is also a classic in showing how a completely fresh technique had to be developed to ferret out the kingpin.

The profits of the heroin traffic can be so great, with the price of the drug soaring from a mere $50 a kilo in the poppy fields of Turkey to $500,000 or more on the streets of America, and the penalties for capture so severe, that shoot-outs are often inevitable. And anyone working for a syndicate knows that the penalty for squealing is death.

A Tough Racket

Narcotics smugglers expect no breaks and give none. In one three-year period, for example, the Bureau of Narcotics and Dangerous Drugs lost no less than 11 agents killed in the line of duty. Countless informers vanished, never to be heard of again, and there is little doubt what happened to them. Here is a strong clue. Not many years ago a customs agent in Texas received a small package from Mexico that contained the personal papers of one of his undercover informants. There was a terse note with them. "Here are his papers. He made one phone call too much. Our regrets to his widow. Gracias." At least they said "thank you."

No one knows the rewards—and the hazards—of drug smuggling better than the smugglers working out of Marseilles, the capital of the heroin traffic. This bustling French seaport is the ideal drug-running center. It has excellent sea links all along the Mediterranean, particularly to Turkey where the opium grows, and to Beirut through which much of it is initially marketed. Marseilles, moreover, is the headquarters of a

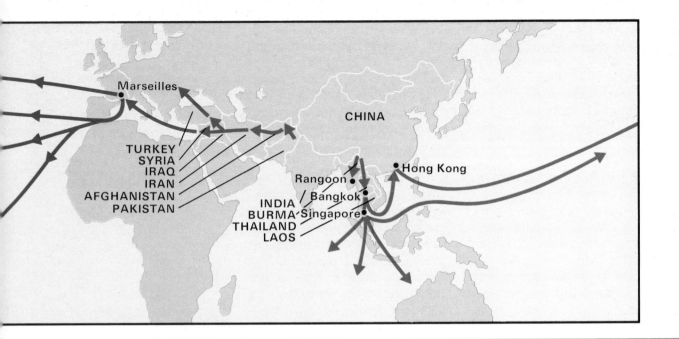

Corsican criminal brotherhood just as tough and ruthless as the Mafia, if less publicized. Like the first Mafia gangsters, the Corsicans came from a poverty striken Mediterranean island. While the Mafiosi boarded the ships from Sicily to the United States, the Corsicans took the ferry to Marseilles in search of fame and fortune. The preferred formula: as little of the former and as much of the latter as possible. There is an old saying in Corsica that when a boy is born his father flips a coin. If it comes down heads, his son will be a policeman, if it comes down tails he will be a criminal—and if it lands on its edge he will work. The narcotics enforcement agents of the world believe that Corsican coins seem to come down tails more often than chance would suggest.

The Corsicans' grip on the Marseilles underworld is complete. They control the waterfront, prostitution, gambling, and protection. They are a tight-knit group constantly suspicious of outsiders and totally loyal to their own.

The international traffic in Turkish and Middle Eastern heroin was built up by Corsicans dealing with Corsicans. All of them are insiders. Any newcomer trying to buy heroin in Marseilles is cold-shouldered—and may even be turned over to the police by the Corsicans themselves. A long standing offer of $30,000 made by the Americans for a tip-off leading to the seizure of a laboratory has never been taken up.

Cracking open such a tight-knit fraternity was almost impossible for many years. Part of the difficulty was that the French themselves did not have a domestic drugs problem, so there was no strong local pressure to bust the smugglers. The American undercover agents of the Bureau of Narcotics and Dangerous Drugs had no legal authority in France. The best they could do

Below: in a hot dry field, a farmer cuts around the fat green pods of the opium poppies, left to swell after the bright petals have fallen. The cut frees the sap, which oozes down the stalk and within a few days dries to a sticky gum. It contains about 10 to 18 percent morphine—the vital element.

was to glean intelligence and pass it on to the French police, hoping they would make the arrests. It became a matter of diplomacy as much as detection. But even if drug traffickers were arrested in France, they received only a five-year sentence. Most Corsican gangsters, knowing that even inside there was no safety for squealers, took their sentences without a murmur rather than help either the French or American agents.

A Job for Trained Chemists

For years Marseilles had flourished as a drug manufacturing center. It is an ideal place for the clandestine drug laboratories, because an essential reagent needed to transform morphine base—the raw product from Turkey—into pure heroin is acetic anhydride, a chemical widely used in making perfume. The great perfume making center of France is in Grasse, just a few miles inland from Marseilles. Unscrupulous chemists working in the perfume industry can easily moonlight making heroin— and many do. The job calls for trained technicians of high skill and concentration because acetic anhydride is explosive, and a chemist can easily blow himself up if he makes his mixture incorrectly. A quiet villa in the country is ideal.

The chemists themselves have no idea who employs them. At most they know the one man who brings them the morphine base and collects the finished heroin. They are paid cash on a job basis. While they do not have a piece of the action, the chemists are not exempt from the strict code of silence surrounding every deal. Even suspicion of the slightest disloyalty could mean a death sentence. Take Jean Galuzzi, for instance. He was a chemist in a secret laboratory. One day the police raided the villa in which he worked and arrested two fellow chemists, Georges Calmet and Albert Vasan. Galuzzi was not there for the simple reason that he had stayed at home with a cold, but he made the fatal error of not phoning in to report his illness. The next morning he was found shot dead. Had he actually tipped off the police and then conveniently stayed at home when they made their raid? Was it coincidence that he caught a cold on the unlucky day? It is doubtful that the killers cared about the answer. Galuzzi was a risk, and he was eliminated.

Keeping the location of the laboratories secret is of utmost importance to a drug smuggling outfit. Captured couriers can be replaced, but the discovery of a laboratory eliminates the key source of supply. This is true of any commercial organization. Delivery men are replaceable, but the factory that produces the product is not. Each syndicate usually has its own laboratory, and sometimes two or more, to produce enough pure heroin for its own needs. If a few extra kilos are needed, the bosses will discreetly shop around and buy some from another organization with a temporary surplus. The hurdle between supply and market is, of course, the Atlantic. By the late 1960s as much as

Right: two heroin chemists, Albert Veran and his assistant Georges Calmet. They were arrested when police raided the small and modest villa that concealed their laboratory.

Below: the Marseilles harbor, teeming with small craft. The city has long been the crucial point in the heroin trail. One agent, John Ingersoll, described the drug trade as an hourglass. The broad base of supply lies in the Near and Middle East; the broad base of distribution is in the United States; the waist between is Marseilles.

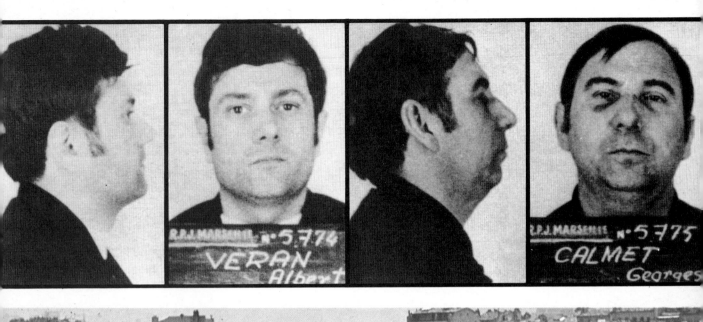

VERAN Albert — R.P.J. MARSEILLE N° 5774

CALMET Georges — P.P.J. MARSEILLE N° 5775

10,000 kilos of heroin had to be moved from France to the United States each year.

The first real evidence that the Corsicans were no longer relying entirely on individual mules, but were sending the heroin to the United States hidden in air freight, came when a French narcotics agent got a whisper about some dope hidden in a shipment of electrical equipment. The word was that the Corsican Paul Chastagnier was the man behind it. The French alerted the American narcotics agents in Paris. They passed the word on to New York. There agents began the dreary task of checking thousands of airline passengers to see if Chastagnier had entered the United States, when, and where.

The picture they put together in three months of painstaking enquiry was that Chastagnier was delivering oscilloscopes—instruments that turn a fluctuating electric current into visible traces on a tube much like that in a TV set. They were sent to a New York firm, Foreign Trade Representations Inc. At that stage investigators still did not know that Chastagnier and his confederates had been putting two half-kilo packets of heroin inside each oscilloscope before shipment. Chastagnier was so confident of the success of this trick that he had actually filled an initial order for 500 of the machines from a small electronics firm—enough to ship slightly more than 500 kilos of heroin into the United States. A dozen oscilloscopes had already made the Atlantic crossing, and the heroin had been safely delivered to the buyer. When a French narcotic agent found out that Chastagnier had another dozen instruments ready for shipment, it was time to take a closer look.

Heroin by Air Freight

The first six instruments in the new batch were consigned by air freight to New York from Orly Airport in Paris. When they arrived, customs agents opened them up and found packets of heroin among the circuitry. The agents carefully replaced the packages, and arranged for their speedy delivery by a customs agent posing as the delivery man. Meanwhile in Paris, Chastagnier was back at Orly with another load of six oscilloscopes. While he was still making out the air freight documents, the French police grabbed him—a hasty action that nearly blew the whole plan. Word of his arrest and the name of the New York firm to which the oscilloscopes were sent leaked to the French press. But the oscilloscopes already in New York, which were to be the basis of the arrests, had not even been delivered when the phone rang on the desk of George Varsa, manager of Foreign Trade Representations Inc. It was a French reporter who asked, "Have you any comment to make on the arrest of Paul Chastagnier in Paris?" Varsa hung up in terror.

A few minutes later a delivery van pulled up outside his office. Outside all looked peaceful; he didn't see the narcotics agents who had the street staked out. They were lying low hoping he

Right: the interior of a secret laboratory for converting morphine base into heroin. Although the process does not require elaborate equipment, it is a fairly dangerous procedure, and a careless chemist runs some danger of blowing himself up with his materials.

Below: the peaceful villa where Veran and Calmet were picked up in their conversion lab.

might lead them to the actual buyer. In fact, Varsa had no idea who the buyer was. His firm was merely a convenient drop for the heroin until the buyer was ready to take it. As he wandered the streets aimlessly, not sure what to do, the agent tailing him finally arrested him for fear of losing him. For Varsa, the frightened and now regretful middleman, it was almost a relief. For the narcotics agents it was a stop-gap action, but not a victory because the key man had eluded the net.

The oscilloscopes affair showed the enforcement agents what they were up against. Air freight comes into the United States by the tens of tons, day and night; there is no conceivable way to check it all. Drug traffickers, who most certainly were dispatching some of it, could enter the United States "clean," and simply supervise the sale. The only hope was a tip in France or the occasional lucky break.

The next big haul was just such a break. A cleaner going over a TWA Boeing 707 at Washington's Dulles Airport found a black nylon stocking stuffed sausagelike with white powder. It was concealed inside the used towel container of one of the plane's toilets. He alerted an airport customs agent who went to have a look. The stocking contained six kilos of heroin—a potentially high profit sausage for the gang who put it on the streets. Who was going to collect it? The plane had just come in from Europe and was scheduled to fly on to Denver within minutes.

Customs men had no time for elaborate plans. They swiftly

Above: part of the enormous 430 kilo heroin seizure made by French narcotics police on the shrimp boat *Caprice des Temps*, captured just out of Marseilles. Said to be bound for the shrimp grounds off Brazil, it was actually heading for Miami, where it would unload its undeclared cargo.

substituted epsom salts for most of the heroin. When the plane took off an agent was sitting in a rear seat near the toilet. Throughout the three-hour flight the agent went into the toilet as soon as any passenger came out, and felt to see if the heroin sausage was still there. Just before the landing in Denver a passenger went into the toilet with a briefcase. When the agent checked on him, the sausage had gone. A few minutes later the Boeing landed in Denver. The customs agents, having spotted the courier, was hard on his heels as he immediately checked in for a flight back to New York. Attempts to trail him there and catch the delivery failed, but the mule was arrested. Under interrogation, it turned out that he had regularly been picking up the heroin sausages on internal flights.

The gambit was almost foolproof. During the transatlantic flight from Paris, the heroin sausage was hidden in the used towel container. The courier who hid it got off the plane in Washington and went through customs clean. When the plane took off on its domestic leg, the second mule was on board to pick up the sausage. Since there are no customs or baggage checks on passengers deplaning from internal flights, he could walk off without any check in Denver. The ruse, it turned out, had been used several times a week for some months. No one ever worked out how much heroin had come that way, although it may have been as much as 500 kilos. Except for a cleaner doing his job thoroughly, it might still be going on.

The uncovering of this subterfuge, and the swift exposure of the real cargo inside Paul Chastagnier's oscilloscopes, were key reasons why the empire of Auguste Ricord grew so rapidly. Because it was getting increasingly difficult to send heroin

directly into the United States, the indirect route via Ricord's
Paris-Nice Motel in Paraguay proved much easier for a while.
Agents were expecting the drugs to come in directly from
Europe, but they were being outflanked.

Any smuggling syndicate finds that it is crucial to, as they
call it, have as many "lines open" as possible. With the heat on
air passengers and air freight, the Marseilles men hit on a new
gimmick: sending the heroin across the ocean in a specially converted boat. They reckoned that no one would pay much attention to a small shrimp boat that made occasional trips across the
Atlantic in search of Caribbean shrimp. Soon a 60-ton shrimper,
Caprice des Temps, embarked from Marseilles for the first of a
number of voyages. The curious thing about the *Caprice des
Temps* was that she seemed to have bad luck with her fishing.
She always came back with a small catch. More curiously, the
captain and crew spent much of their time in Miami. Were they
enjoying the high life of Miami Beach or were they . . . ?

French customs agents finally decided they would take a look
at the *Caprice des Temps* out at sea. They were really playing a
hunch that she was involved in smuggling cigarettes around the
Mediterranean. A customs launch stopped the shrimper one day
in 1971 as she sailed out of Marseilles harbor ostensibly for
shrimp grounds off Brazil, and put an armed boarding party
aboard. They searched the boat from stem to stern, but found
nothing illegal or even suspicious. They were just about to depart
when an alert officer noted that the concrete ballast in the hold
was not exactly level. "What's under the ballast?" they asked
the shrimper's captain, Marcel Boucan. Captain Boucan made
no reply. He jumped overboard, and for good reason. Beneath

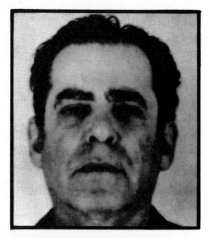

Above: Jean-Baptiste Croce (top) and Joseph Mari, after their capture by the Marseilles waterfront narcotics squad. They were partners who headed one of the Corsican rings.

the ballast the customs men found 420 kilos of pure heroin—the biggest heroin haul of all time and worth a fortune. Marcel Boucan was picked up the following morning as he staggered ashore near Marseilles. During his interrogation he admitted that on several previous voyages the *Caprice des Temps'* real cargo had also been heroin.

Boucan was merely a high-powered and highly paid mule. The real organizers were still remote. But their untouchable status could not last forever. For many years American agents working in France had a pretty good idea who the real men behind the French Connection were. The hard task was to get enough solid evidence. To persuade the French police to act on it was even more difficult.

End of the French Connection
The situation gradually changed, however. First, cases like the *Caprice des Temps* meant that the French could no longer ignore what was going on. Almost 1000 kilos of pure heroin was being loaded in one of their ports. That was entirely different from a small time Corsican gangster stepping off a plane in New York with a few kilos taped to his body. Secondly, and perhaps more important, the French suddenly found they had a domestic heroin addiction problem. The success of the Americans in catching couriers across the Atlantic meant that quantities of heroin were backing up in Marseilles and being filtered into the French market. Previously there had been a few hundred addicts in France. Now suddenly there were 6000 or 7000. Their growing concern made the French authorities work out a new procedure with the Americans to crack down on the traffickers. Prison sentences were raised from five to 20 years. The extra 15 years had a telling effect on the code of silence. Although underlings were willing to do five years time, the threat of 20 caused information to flow. The Marseilles narcotics squad—which at one time consisted of only a handful of men who had to borrow cars from the police pool—was increased to 150. They were supplied with two-way radios and a fleet of baker's and laundry trucks from which they could carry out discreet observation.

Gradually, hard diligent police work paid off. The net was tightened around the real ringleaders. One evening outside a bar on the Marseilles waterfront narcotics squad operatives arrested at gun point two men: Jean-Baptiste Croce and Joseph Mari. Croce was the proprietor of a fashionable café in the Coriscan city of Bastia and the owner of a luxury yacht, appropriately named *L'Escapade*. Mari, his partner, was a prosperous Marseilles bar owner. Both had long been suspected of being *gros bonnets* (big chiefs) in the narcotics racket, but until then they had been considered untouchable. No longer. Croce got 18 years in jail and, in all, sentences of 95 years were handed out to members of his gang, most of whom were taken during the general crackdown. Mari himself died in prison before he was sentenced.

One man, however, was still at liberty: Joseph Marro. Ostensibly he ran a flourishing wallpaper business in Marseilles, but in actuality he was the financial backer of Croce and Mari's heroin empire. Marro was a gambler who lived in a luxurious flat in Paris. He explained his high living by saying that he borrowed money from his son—though why his son should have so much money no one knew. Marro eluded the initial police dragnet and escaped to Switzerland where he hid for almost two years. One day, however, a police informer phoned. Marro was coming back to France secretly to attend his sister's funeral. Narcotics agents swiftly picked up his trail and cornered him in a villa near Marseilles. Marro had gone there apparently to try to soothe the owner of the villa, who had accused Marro of encouraging his wife's infidelity with one Edmond Tailler, a heroin smuggler arrested in New York. For all his caution in his heroin dealings, Marro was brought to justice through the sexual adventures of one of his men.

No one expected the breakup of one major gang to halt the heroin flow, but it did prove to everyone that even the toughest of Corsican gangs was vulnerable to the combined pressure of French and American law enforcement. Moreover, their exposure came just as the United States persuaded Turkey to stop all opium production for a trial period of two years in return for compensation of $35 million. Although the Marseilles operators had stockpiled a large supply of morphine base in advance to keep their labs going, it began to look as if the closedown of their basic source of supply meant that Marseilles' days as the headquarters of heroin were numbered.

That hope, however, was short-lived. In 1974 Turkey announced that the suspension of opium production would not continue. The farmers of Afyon Province had suffered too much from the stoppage of the basic crop they had grown for centuries, and the notion that wheat, barley, and other crops could be substituted was not correct. The climate in central Turkey was too harsh. So early in 1975 the farmers brought in their first opium harvest for three years. While the Turks claimed to have tightened up their controls so that there could be no excess illicit production for the black market, few believed them. The task of policing some 200,000 farms in remote Turkish valleys is impossible.

The success of the Americans in cracking the French Connection and in persuading the Turks to stop opium growing for a while did nothing to stop the demand for heroin. It simply opened up opportunities for heroin to come from Mexico, where a rather inferior poppy producing brown heroin is grown, and, above all, from the Far East. The French Connection was replaced by an Oriental one.

The opium poppy is grown in the "Golden Triangle" of northern Thailand, Laos, and the Shan States of Burma—hot hilly country that is impossible to police properly. For years the

Above: Kemalettin Gazeezoglu, governor of Afyon province in Turkey. Afyon, which means "opium," is the country's chief producer of the opium poppy. American attempts to stop all opium production in Turkey by a program of economic aid for other crops failed. It was said that the substitute crops would not grow in the Afyon region.

37

Right: a Yao girl, member of one of the hill tribes in the Golden Triangle. Her necklace, bought with the proceeds of her family's opium harvest, is of solid silver. During the opium gathering season, farmers sleep with their guns in a hut right in the poppy field—for a few weeks the field is exceedingly valuable property indeed.

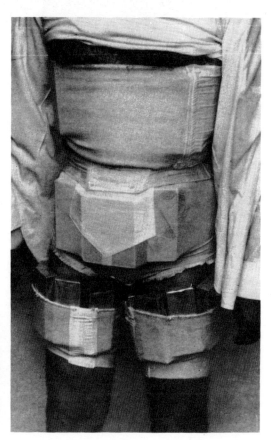

Far left: a traveler from Bangkok who arrived in Hong Kong and was stopped by customs agents. They thought he looked rather suspiciously bulky.

Left: beneath the business suit were these packages of morphine base, neatly taped around the smuggler's body.

Below: in Asia, heroin is identified by various brand names. This 999 is supposed to indicate high quality, just as gold bars are stamped 999 to show purity.

opium produced there had been primarily for Asian addicts. It had been smuggled down to Bangkok, from there to Hong Kong or Singapore, and then to Japan, one of the biggest black markets outside the United States. Most of it has been prettily packaged. To emphasize the quality of his morphine blocks, one Chinese smuggler took to stamping them 999, just as gold bars are stamped 999 to confirm their purity. Soon morphine blocks throughout the Far East bore similar stamps attesting their quality. The popular brands were OK, AAA, Dragon, and Two Tigers. The OK brand of smoking opium came in a colorful wrapping showing a crane perched on a willow tree and gazing down at a junk cruising on an azure sea.

The Vietnam war changed all that. Countless American servicemen found they could set up profitable links with friends back home to supply drugs. The vast armada of United States aircraft ferrying men and equipment to and from the war zone provided an ideal smuggling route. It was impossible in wartime to submit all the aircraft to meticulous searches.

From the outset there was one crucial difference in the war-stimulated drug traffic from Asia. Unlike the closely knit Corsican fraternity handling the Turkey–France–United States flow, the business in Southeast Asia was up for grabs. There was no natural racial link, which most criminals prefer.

The motley assortment of smugglers involved made it much easier for American narcotics agents and their informers to in-

Right: a police launch glides through Hong Kong harbor after a suspicious junk. The harbor is full of picturesque but very practical craft with a seemingly infinite variety of clever places to hide an illegal cargo of the valuable morphine base.

Below: sometimes Hong Kong narcotics agents strike lucky. They located this store of 999 morphine packages inside hollowed-out teak logs that had arrived from Bangkok.

filtrate the smuggling groups, something that was virtually impossible with the Corsicans. They were helped a great deal by a number of expatriate French adventurers living in Southeast Asia, who had been making a living doing everything from smuggling gold to holding up banks. Many of these men had been in Saigon, Phnom Penh, and Bangkok ever since the French defeat in Vietnam in the early 1950s.

One Success Story

One of the most daring of these French adventerors actually took to smuggling morphine base from Bangkok to Hong Kong with the connivance of American agents in an effort to identify who was really organizing the traffic there. One Saturday afternoon in Bangkok, a Chinese drug trafficker handed him 20 kilos of morphine base, which he hid carefully in a briefcase. He drove out to the airport and took a Cathay Pacific flight to Hong Kong, under the watchful eyes of an American narcotics agent who sat across the aisle. At Hong Kong's Kai Tak Airport he went easily through customs, whose staff knew what was going on, and took a taxi to the Star Ferry that chugs across from Kowloon to Hong Kong Island. American and Hong Kong police agents were close on his tail the whole time.

The Frenchman had been instructed in Bangkok that during the 10-minute ferry crossing he was to make delivery to a man

who would identify himself by a code word. Sure enough a
Chinese laborer brushed up against him on the boat and
whispered the identifying code; the briefcase was transferred.
The Frenchman stepped off the ferry, walked across the terminal, and took the next boat back to Kowloon. There he
hastened to the airport and boarded the next flight back to
Bangkok. All this was according to the plan laid out by the
Chinese organizer of the run. Meanwhile plainclothes narcotics
agents of the Hong Kong police were right behind the laborer
with the briefcase as he left the ferry terminal and headed for an
apartment near the Cat Street antiques market. As he made the
delivery inside, the agents rushed in to arrest the mule and his
buyer. When word of the seizure got back to Bangkok the
Frenchman had to do some fast explaining to his Chinese contact, but he was able to convince him that the tip-off must have
come at the Hong Kong end. He claimed it was not he, but the
courier there who had been fingered. "Even so," he admitted
much later, "I carried my gun with me night and day for a year
after that."

The technique of setting themselves up as heroin buyers was
widely used by narcotics agents in ferreting out the Oriental
Connection, an obvious but highly dangerous method. A narcotics agent is often sure who the big suppliers are, but lacks the
hard evidence; or he may know who the intermediary is, but not
the kingpin. The only way to get such vital information is for

The $30 Million Deal

The mercenary army of a modern war lord escorts an opium caravan out of Burma hill country.

the agent himself to pretend he wants to buy heroin. It is a game as subtle as fly fishing, but deadly. The agent must have a perfect cover; he must have the right background; and he must be able to offer substantial amounts of cash.

The bait was often huge, as can be seen from an operation at the American end of the Asian heroin traffic. The two men who one day approached Kenneth Kahnkit Huie, a self-styled "mayor of Chinatown" in New York, were prepared to go as high as $200,000 cash for just 44 kilos of pure heroin that Huie had shipped in from Chinese connections in Southeast Asia. They offered to pay the money in $50 and $100 bills, and deliver it to Huie on Gold Street in lower Manhattan at precisely 9:00 p.m. one summer night. Huie agreed.

On the appointed night the two buyers drove up a little early in a glossy Cadillac and parked outside a hospital. The street seemed quiet enough except for an emergency crew working by an open manhole cover a short way off, and there was no sign of life from a windowless minibus parked across from the Cadillac.

Promptly at 9:00 p.m. Huie and a friend, Tim Lok, came strolling up the street. They stopped near the Cadillac. The two men inside got out, greeted Huie and went around to open the trunk. They showed him the $200,000 bundled according to instructions and placed in an attaché case. Huie, satisfied, set off

In 1975 the United States was offered a curious deal. The opium smugglers of the Shan States of Burma—part of the nearly impenetrable hill country that borders on China, Laos, and Thailand—offered to sell their entire crop to the United States for roughly $30 million. Normally, the Shan area produces about a third of the world's black market opium. The street price of their crop, converted into heroin, would work out at about $30 billion. So the United States was offered what appears to be a bargain in more ways than one.

The smugglers who made the offer are part of the resistance armies living and fighting in the Burma hills since the present government was established by *coup d'etat* in 1962. In their desperately poor area, the Shans have only one cash crop: opium. The country is dry and hard, and very little will grow there. One thing that does flourish is the opium poppy, and it is the proceeds from the opium harvest that arm and sustain the Shans' challenge to the central Burmese government for control of their region.

The opium is carried down from the Shan hills mainly by tribesmen walking for up to a week, each one carrying about 25 kilos. They dump the raw opium in Thai border villages, and collect $5–$12 a kilo, which almost certainly represents their only cash income for the year. Then they return to their villages, and the opium moves on through Thailand to Bangkok, and from there out to the world.

The Shan opium exporters, after a brisk series of skirmishes to establish who was going to control both the trade and the discussions with the Americans, offered a most interesting set of proposals. They agreed to sign a treaty that would promise the end of the opium trade entirely once peace and order was restored to the Shan States. In the meantime, they were prepared to sell the annual Shan opium crop, amounting to about 400–500 tons, to the United States at a fixed price; to prevent smuggling; and to invite American inspectors into the opium region.

The first attempt at negotiation was abortive. The Shan leader was tricked into a Thai police helicopter and arrested.

The second attempt led to a meeting between the Shans and a Congressional Sub-Committee, meeting secretly in one of Bangkok's luxurious hotels. The congressmen were definitely interested in the proposals of the Shans.

Unfortunately, the State Department was not. They argued that the removal of Shan opium from the black market would create a shortage and raise prices, which would stimulate more people to grow opium. They also felt that the Burmese Army was the best force to use against smuggling, and have delivered helicopters to them to use for narcotics prevention. Some skeptical congressmen asked how the State Department could be certain that the helicopters would not be used for military purposes, when even the American ambassador is not allowed in the opium area. They answered that they accepted Burmese assurances for the proper use of the equipment.

In the end, the State Department won. The Shans went back to the hills, and their opium continues its tortuous way down the hill trails to the wide river winding through Bangkok, to the heroin laboratories of Hong Kong, to the waiting addicts on the streets in many cities around the world.

with one of the buyers to collect his heroin. They ended up in a Chinese sportswear store where Huie opened a cardboard box to reveal 14 plastic bags of heroin. Still cautious, Huie and the buyer taxied back to Gold Street, while the owner of the store, Guan Chowtok, followed them in his car with the heroin. On the way Chowtok became nervous and dumped the heroin on an empty lot near Brooklyn Bridge. He then drove to Gold Street without the heroin. A furious argument ensued. The buyer had the money and demanded that the Chinese complete the delivery.

Finally everyone piled into the Cadillac and Chowtok led them to the Brooklyn Bridge. There beneath the bridge was the cardboard box. The buyer knelt down to check it. "This is the package, this is the package," he said loudly. Narcotics agents closed in all around as the message went out over a concealed radio inside his shirt. They had followed every second of the maneuvers from the moment their two undercover agents had met the Chinese on Gold Street, but had been unable to move until the actual transfer of the heroin took place. The three Chinese were led away at gunpoint, furious that they had walked into the trap laid by the narcotics agents. But that is the essence of the narcotics traffic: it runs on the ball bearings of bribery and deceit.

Peddlers in Pot
3

There was a time when any tourist stepping off the ferryboat from Spain to Tangier was greeted on the pier by a gaggle of guides offering tours of the Kasbah or introductions to other mysterious delights of Morocco. Such carefree days are gone. Now everybody runs the gauntlet of an x-ray machine that peers into all their baggage to make sure they aren't bringing in a rifle to assassinate Morocco's King Hassan. After half a dozen attempts to murder the king, no chances are taken that some hired killer may slip into the country on a Jackal-type mission. But once the visitor has passed through these precautionary measures, the guides are still there. What they offer, however, has changed—for Kasbah read *kif*.

Kif means peace and tranquility, and is of course that tall straggly plant with narrow spiky leaves covered with a fuzz of tiny hairs, known botanically and officially by narcotics agents as *Cannabis sativa*. Like Morocco, most countries have a local name for it. The Egyptians call it *hashish*, "best of herbs;" the Indians know it as *charas*; the Jamaicans as *ganga*; and the Mexicans christened it *marijuana*. Most young people around the world who smoke it simply call it "pot."

Pot has become one of Morocco's best export items in recent years. Those eager guides grabbing the visitors by the arm as they search for a taxi or look for the road signs to steer their vehicles out of town toward the ancient cities of Fez or Meknes have all the right connections. They can provide kif by the kilo, or even by the ton—and at competitive prices. In Morocco it costs anything between $60 and $100 a kilo, depending on how good a bargain can be struck. The street value of that kilo in New York, London, Amsterdam, or Copenhagen is anything between $800 and $1500, depending on quality and market supply.

Tangier is merely the outpost. The capital of kif and the center of business is Ketama, a tiny village located in the region of Rif 150 miles to the southeast. There is a good road most of the way. The only gauntlets to be run are the checkpoints of the Royal Moroccan Gendarmerie set up on the outskirts of most villages. The police lay down two lines of spikes halfway across the road, making all motor traffic weave between them at a

Above: smoking pot, now an accepted social custom among the young. Its great popularity increases the demand for a drug that—so far—can only be supplied by the cannabis smugglers.

Right: the ones who had their fingers burned—young Americans in a Spanish jail. They must often wait up to a year for trial, and the minimum sentence is six years and one day for any drug smuggling charge.

Right: the flourishing fields of young marijuana plants near the highway leading to Ketama, Morocco, a small village with only one crop to sell. There buying and selling hashish is not illegal—the buyers only move to the other side of the law when they attempt to take it out of Morocco with them.

Below: a Moroccan peasant at work preparing raw hashish, the brown or black substance that is formed from the resin of the straggly marijuana plant.

snail's pace. That enables the police to take a good look at everyone inside and wave down any suspicious types for a check of identity papers. Most foreign visitors are cheerfully waved through; the alert is for potential assassins, not kif buyers.

Approaching Ketama, even the road signs show the local specialty: "00–1–2–500 m" says a white sign. To the initiate it means that kif of top quality (00), second quality (1), and third quality (2) is available 500 meters away. That is only the beginning of the hard sell. Soon a couple of young men astride a motor scooter roar up alongside any stranger's car and, keeping a parallel course, start offering pot.

Ketama: Kif City

The main street of the little village itself is almost awash with everyone from tots to old men offering anything from reefers to one-kilo packs of kif. In the fields all around cannabis plants thrive—acres of them. The cultivation is open and apparently legal. In Morocco, where most people are Muslims and forbidden to use alcohol, kif has been smoked for centuries. "It's become part of the life here" says one local. "A Moroccan's relaxation is kif, an American's is a martini. Anyway up in the Rif nothing else will grow."

The one-, two-, even five-kilo transactions are small potatoes. The real action in Ketama takes place in one of a few discreet villas. There the buyers recline on long low sofas, sipping highly sweetened glasses of mint tea and sampling delicate pastries. The talk is not of a few reefers, but of kif by the ton. The smuggling of cannabis from Morocco to the capitals of Europe is

Right: a young tourist buying
hashish from a street vendor in
a Moroccan bazaar. Kif, as it
is called there, has been a
part of Moroccan life for long
centuries, and is not at all
illegal for Moroccans. It is
the states surrounding Morocco
—mainly Algeria and Spain—
that have taken a hard line in
order to stop the smugglers and
their drugs from coming across.

no longer a matter of a few hippies bringing back a little pot for themselves and their friends. It has become a highly organized, professional traffic worth several million dollars each year.

The first official alert to how well planned the business had become came one day early in 1973 as the car ferry *Eagle* docked at Southampton on England's south coast. Two sharp-eyed British immigration men, waiting to check passports, noticed a passenger carefully tapping the walls of a trailer and peering underneath it just before it was driven off the ship. The passenger then went back to his own Jaguar to drive ashore. The immigration officers tipped off customs officials, who stopped both the Jaguar and the Rover 2000 pulling the trailer. The customs men took the trailer completely apart. In an operation lasting over eight hours, they stripped off the walls, took up the floor, and removed the sink and the cupboards. Tucked away in every conceivable niche they found neatly wrapped and numbered blocks of cannabis. Many of the packets had been cut to fit a small space, and were taped into place. The total haul was 400 kilos worth, the equivalent of $700,000 on the market in Britain. Hiding it had been a major undertaking. The two men charged with smuggling it, Maurice Tudor and Victor Berrill, were said to have spent a week stripping the trailer down to the frame, stowing the drug, and rebuilding the vehicle.

The *Eagle* seizure was just the beginning. Over the next few months more than 9000 kilos of pot worth over $19 million were seized by British customs authorities, a clear indication that the days when the pot-smoking student brought in a couple of ounces in his knapsack were over. The big-time operators had moved onto the scene.

The fight against this blossoming traffic was helped by the

Above: in 1974 a family came back to Britain from a vacation in Tangiers, hauling this trailer. They passed through customs easily enough, but Joseph Delgado, the driver, was so nervous that he drove straight into a wall on leaving. Customs officials got interested, came to investigate, and found nearly $500,000 worth of hash hidden in the roof of the car.

creation of a National Drugs Intelligence Unit, centered at Scotland Yard and combining the technical resources and agents of customs, police, and immigration. The picture they were able to piece together with the help of Interpol was that the launching platform for pot smuggling was either Tangier or Casablanca.

Outwitting Customs

The mules were recruited in coffee bars and discotheques in Amsterdam, Stockholm, Marseilles, Dusseldorf, or London. The initial contact was always discreet. The prospective couriers were asked if they would like a nice vacation by minibus through North Africa with all expenses paid plus a "present" at the end if they did "a little job." Drugs were rarely mentioned. Should the potential mule show interest, he would be asked if he had a girl friend to go along. If not, he was told to get one to make things look more natural. The reward was either some of the kif itself, or anything between $2500 and $5000 in cash after a safe delivery. For many youngsters the prospect of a free week or two in the sun was all too tempting. They could even bone up on the wiles of pot smuggling by reading *The Truckers Bible*. This handbook was a mine of useful suggestions on outwitting customs officials and bribing one's way to freedom if caught.

The booklet pointed out: "Try and be professional. Hundreds of small-time traffickers are in jail because they underestimated the intelligence of customs officers. They are trained, prejudiced and suspicious and for the most part good at their job. It's up to you to exploit their system if you can."

Potential smugglers were advised to have their hair cut and to

Left below: the stripped-down trailer showing the secret compartment under the roof where an impressive quantity of cannabis could be hidden out of sight of customs men.

Below: the piles of cannabis, neatly wrapped, which the customs agents discovered tucked inside the secret roof cache installed in the trailer.

Above: two issues of an underground publication, the *Trucker's Bible*, **which offers potential smugglers helpful information on how to evade the attentions of customs officers at borders.**

be neat and tidy—"to avoid a hippie appearance." If their existing passport photographs showed them looking like freaks, they were advised to lose the passport and get a new one with a more dignified photograph in it. A passport with many entry stamps for the known pot-growing countries—Afghanistan, Nepal, or Lebanon—should also be replaced.

As for concealing the drugs, the handbook warned that customs men knew all about such hiding places as spare tires and headlights. It was best to have a special compartment built in the vehicle before leaving home. The cargo of pot should be picked up at the rendezvous in another vehicle, and later transferred to the one used for delivery. If drugs were found, the smuggler should insist from the outset that he had never seen them before, and that he was clearly the innocent victim of a plant. Bribes might be appropriate in some countries at lonely border posts only, but must be offered before any police paperwork commenced.

Whatever confidence this booklet may have given budding mules, it was certainly not enough to help many of them outwit the authorities, who were even better informed than its authors dreamed. The routes were all too obvious, and the fact that many couriers were posing as family groups returning from vacations did not fool the customs men for a moment.

At first the favorite landing point in Europe was Algeciras, the little whitewashed Spanish port opposite the Rock of Gibraltar. It is just two hours on the car ferry from Tangier. Smugglers dubbed it "the marijuana gateway to Europe." They came off the ferry by the score with cannabis hidden in false gas tanks, beneath double floors, and in hollow mudguards. There is a story that one ingenious fellow even sprayed a highly con-

Left: one of the cardinal rules stated in the *Trucker's Bible* is "to avoid a hippie appearance." This young man found his exotic apparel alerted the Spanish customs agent, who made a meticulous search of everything he carried. As it happened, no drugs were found.

Below: Howard Fowler, one of the many young Americans who have been picked up in Spain with a load of Moroccan hash. Fowler had his 30-odd kilos hidden in a rented car. At the time of this picture, he had served about half of his six-year sentence in a Spanish jail.

centrated liquid cannabis all over the inside of his car, let it dry, and then sprayed paint on top. He intended to scrape off the paint-and-pot mixture and reconstitute it. But the sweet sickly smell of the drug came through the paint, and an alert customs man, putting his head through the car window, sniffed the familiar scent.

In the space of a few months Spanish customs men, fully aware of what was going on, arrested 55 smugglers and slapped them into prison. They had to wait for up to a year before coming to trial to receive sentences of one to ten years. The deterrent was enough to make the organizers look for alternative routes. A close look at the map of North Africa revealed a cunning alternative. Instead of driving from Ketama to Tangier, the mules simply turned east and drove along the Moroccan coast to the little town of Oujda close to the Algerian border. Oujda was already a famous smuggling town from which tons of gold jewelery are smuggled into Algeria. In Oujda it is relatively easy to arrange an undisturbed crossing into Algeria. Once over the border it is a short drive to Algiers and regular car ferries to Marseilles.

The new route seemed safe because there was little history of drug smuggling from tightly controlled Algeria into France. But once again the smugglers failed to take into account the increasing sophistication of the intelligence network of police and customs in Europe and North Africa. The *Sureté Nationale*, the Algerian national police force, soon heard what was going on and cracked down hard. In just four months they arrested more than 100 smugglers, both European and American, in 44 vehicles carrying drugs.

Determined to stop the traffic, the Algerian government

enacted a new law giving the death penalty for drug smuggling. They even made it retroactive to include two smugglers caught a few months previously. A Dutchman, Arthur Pouw, who had been arrested with 500 kilos of hashish hidden in a motor boat towed behind his Mercedes, was sentenced to death. So was an Englishman, Harry Calleia. Calleia's sentence was singularly harsh inasmuch as he had not actually been found with drugs. It was a mule alleged to be working for him who had been caught in Algeria. A telegram purporting to come from this courier was sent to Calleia in England. The message was an urgent plea for Calleia to come to Algiers. He took the next plane out, was arrested as he landed, and was charged with conspiring to smuggle drugs. In court he said that he had been tortured to extract a confession.

The Algerian arrests were part of a pattern of close liaison between European and North African police forces. The deputy head of the British Drugs Intelligence Unit even made an unpublicized visit to Algiers to discuss smuggling with the Sureté Nationale. He talked at great length with Semmeache Abdelkader, the deputy director of public safety, and interviewed many of the prisoners. Such face-to-face discussions between senior police intelligence officers had rarely taken place before, but they clearly paid dividends. Smuggling through Algiers promptly stopped. A few months later, Director Abdelkader, reflecting that arrests by his force had dropped from about 30 a month to none, laconically observed that "perhaps word has gotten around."

Just to make sure that no one was getting through the tight net spread in North Africa, the Marseilles drug squad turned out in force to meet incoming ferries from Algiers and Casablanca. On one occasion 60 French police officers met a single car ferry. The searchers handed out polite notices to all passengers saying that they were sorry for the inconvenience, but that 1695 kilograms of drugs had already been seized in the port that year. "Our goal," said the note, "is to stop the traffickers, for drugs threaten the young people of all countries." The search paid off. Two Englishmen were found with drugs in their car.

Left: farmers in Lebanon bring in their hashish harvest near the Lebanese-Syrian border. It is from Lebanon that most hash is sold openly to other Middle East countries. Buyers from the United States and Europe can only make illegal arrangements. Many do, and many are caught.

Right: a dog, especially trained to detect hashish by its characteristic strong sweet smell, checks over a tourist's baggage at a Lebanese border checkpoint.

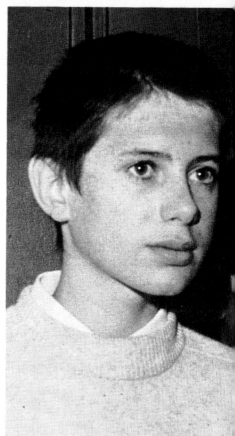

Left: a young American couple on their honeymoon—both only 21 years old—are told by the United States consul in Spain that there is nothing he can do about their six-year jail sentence for drug smuggling. Below: young Timothy Davey, a 14-year-old English boy, was apprehended with drugs in Turkey while on a trip with his family. He was sentenced to six years in prison, but was released after having served 33 months in a Turkish jail.

In the next few weeks, 25 drug mules from North Africa were picked up in Marseilles in a few weeks, including several elderly couples chosen for the job because they were less likely to attract suspicion.

One French detective suggested that older people were being deliberately selected by callous organizers on the theory that, if caught, they might suffer heart attacks and not give away their employers.

The pressure exerted by concerted international police effort made the smuggling bosses much more wary in their selection of mules. Now they began choosing family groups with children, in which only one person would have any idea what was going on.

The Innocent Smugglers

Mrs Frances Martin says that she has no idea how 172 pounds of cannabis came to be welded into the bodywork of her car. She says that she thought she was having the car repaired.

However, she was arrested when she brought the car by ferry into the French port of Sète on June 5, 1975, and she has been in a prison cell since. Her cell is about eight feet by five feet, and after 8:00 pm the lights are turned out, so that all winter through she has a long night with what she calls "beasties." In the morning and afternoon she spends two hours in the prison yard. Two of her friends are a German girl and a French girl who both speak English, and laughed grimly when they heard her story. Both of them claim to have had similar experiences as unwitting smugglers.

Perhaps the court was moved by Mrs Martin's story, because she was originally sentenced to only one year with six months suspended. That is a light sentence for conviction on a drug smuggling charge. But the prosecution successfully appealed, and her sentence now stands at three years. Because she has had tuberculosis and suffers from asthma, the prison governor's wife allows her to keep her asthma inhaler in her cell at night, although it is against regulations.

Mrs Martin is in her late 50s, and feels saddest about the thought that she is spending a time of her life when the years are running out locked in a prison cell. She keeps her morale up by knitting and reading Agatha Christie murder mysteries from the prison bookshelf. And she plans her journey home, lovingly thinking about and going over all the little details. "When I get out of here," she says, "I want to forget that there ever was a country called France."

Was Mrs Martin tricked into smuggling pot? She could well have been. It is known that some smugglers persuade unsuspicious travelers to have their cars serviced in Morocco in order to secrete cannabis in them.

Mrs Frances Martin, British mother of five and a grandmother, was sentenced to three years in a French prison for smuggling pot in her car from Morocco.

Toward the end of the Moroccan vacation, the car would simply go in for servicing for a day or two. Servicing in this case meant the hiding of the pot. Another tactic was for a member of the smuggling gang to make friends with vacationers either before they went to Morocco or while they were there, and then borrow their cars for a couple of days. During that time he would have the hash hidden, and return the car to the innocent family. Back in England he would meet them again and borrow the car again to take the drugs out.

The sad outcome of all these schemes was that the real organizers were rarely caught, and punishment befell the couriers. It was not so much that the organizers were unknown, but that it was tough to get the evidence on them. "We've had a recent case," said a British diplomat in Morocco, "of a young husband and wife who were caught with 62 kilos in a carefully converted caravan [trailer]. He's got two years and a fine of £20,000 [$45,000 at the time], and we're trying to persuade his smuggling employers at least to pay for the fine and his defense."

Coaxing the real organizers out into the open where they can be snared with the evidence requires patience and steady nerve. At the Moroccan end, the levels of protection run so high that the handful of bosses at the very top have little fear of arrest. The real brains, known to the police as "the Godfather," is said to be a wealthy Rabat businessman who provides much of

Above: the large comfortable house in Reading, England, in which a commune developed a lucrative hashish smuggling organization. It was broken by an undercover policeman who infiltrated the smuggling group.

the financing required. He has three principal lieutenants in Ketama. They operate a hash packaging plant that parcels up the drug in plastic bags like sugar for a supermarket, and they have installed special presses to extract a highly concentrated liquid cannabis.

Police Infiltration

Police work can be particularly effective in cracking the European syndicates buying from Morocco. Even that calls for stealthy undercover work, often stretching over many months. An initial tip-off is crucial. One disgruntled courier who had been arrested in Marseilles with hashish in his car suggested that the police pay some attention to a commune occupying a large house in Reading, a town near London. The French police passed the word to Scotland Yard. A few days later a bearded young man, who said his name was Joe, turned up at the "Let it Be" commune. In time, and with all the caution and reticence of the trade, he let it be known that he was a dealer looking for a connection. Several days later Mike Marchington, an Australian living in the commune, told Joe he could let him have 30 kilos of prime Moroccan hashish every three weeks.

Marchington said he had already made several trips, including one with his girl friend Eve Dutton, who also lived in the commune. They had been to Ketama, and had met a Canadian who had all the right connections. Known only as Frank, this Canadian had arranged for $15,000 worth of drugs to be hidden behind the sink of their minibus. Safely back in England, Marchington had lined up another trip for which he recruited a young man from the commune, Jeremy Wing. His fee was to be $2500. Wing had bad luck. He was caught in Algeciras with

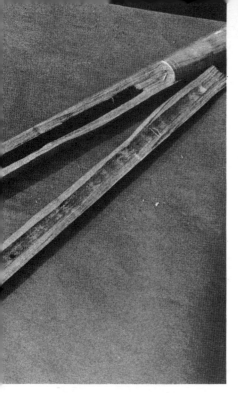

Above: even that symbol of the traditional English summer—the cricket stump—has been used by smugglers. They packed a shipment of cannabis into the hollowed-out stumps that came from Pakistan.
Right: the box of stumps. The customs men point out that tighter security measures, designed primarily to prevent terrorist activity, make detection of smuggled goods easier.

41 kilos of kif and 400 grams of liquid cannabis concealed in his minibus, and put into jail.

Not discouraged, Marchington arranged other trips to Morocco, even asking a Canadian friend to fly over to make one run for a $2500 fee. Another member of the group, Lloyd Samuels, was also bringing in pot, but he told Joe that his source of supply was Jamaica. He could offer up to 1000 kilos at a time at $150,000 or so. Joe seemed like a reliable friend to them all, and he was eager to buy his way into the action. So it was arranged that the money and the dope should be brought together in a cool (safe) house. Late one night Joe went to the safe house with the money. Three members of the gang were there to make the delivery. Right behind Joe came his fellow detectives from the drug squad of Thames Valley police. Joe, it turned out, was really Detective Constable Martin Pritchard. Nine members of the commune were arrested and later sent to prison for periods up to four years. Jeremy Wing languished in a Spanish jail.

Another member of the group decided not to stay around; he jumped his bail and fled to Amsterdam. No doubt he felt at

Above: in the Netherlands the official attitude is permissive. Here hash tea—a highly concentrated liquid form of hashish —is served to customers of the "Lowlands Weed Compagnie," a barge moored in Amsterdam.

home there because Amsterdam is for pot and most soft drugs what Marseilles has long been for the heroin traffic—the crossroads. The Netherlands takes a relaxed attitude to most soft drugs—that is, those claimed to be nonaddictive. In fact the Minister of Health in 1975, Irene Vorrink, is in favor of legalizing the possession of pot. Her young son could even be heard over the radio every Saturday afternoon quoting the latest prices in Dutch guilders: "Nepal, 12 per gram; Morocco, 10.25; Lebanon, 8.50." The small Amsterdam drugs squad mostly turns a blind eye to youngsters found with pot in their possession. They have enough to do trying to control the shoot-outs of an unruly gang of Chinese heroin dealers, who set up shop in Amsterdam marketing "brown sugar"—a brown heroin from Southeast Asia.

Down along the canals of the Amsterdam redlight area, among the live sex shows and dirty movies, cannabis in every shape or form is as easy to come by as a drink or a prostitute. The drug comes into the Netherlands by the ton. Morocco is one prime source of supply. It is also brought in by trucks coming overland from Iran, and by cargo ships from Beirut that rendezvous in the North Sea with private yachts or fishing boats putting out from Dutch ports. Another favorite route is by plane from Southeast Asia to Brussels, then by car in three hours to Amsterdam.

Pot for Pleasure and Profit

The sheer availability of drugs in Amsterdam, and the near absence of controls, makes the city a Mecca both for dropouts in search of a quick reefer, and for dealers from all over Europe in search of a regular source of supply. The industrial cities of Germany are just an hour or two away by car, while Copenhagen and Stockhom are within easy reach by plane and train. The scale of the smuggling is immense. In a single year the West German police arrested 2166 mules on the Netherlands–German border.

The Dutch police can do little about it. There are 130 separate police forces in the Netherlands, and they have little liaison with each other. There is no nationwide drug squad, and Amsterdam's drug squad consists of a mere eight detectives. They cannot make arrests for conspiracy because the Netherlands has no conspiracy laws such as those frequently used in other countries to trap the organizers of drug rackets. They are also forbidden to infiltrate a drug ring. They can act only if the drug is actually offered to them. One government official lamented: "Drugs are flooding in and we are going to drown unless our dykes are made more effective."

Easy access to pot in Amsterdam has lured dealers from across the Atlantic. Until the late 1960s everyone in North America simply smoked marijuana smuggled in from Mexico, but by the early 1970s the United States authorities were seizing as much as $50 million worth of hashish a year, spirited in from Europe.

The first big haul involved $4 million worth of hashish found hidden in the floor of a truck that arrived in San Francisco abroad a freighter from Antwerp. The operators soon came up with a much better idea than that. Ernie Combs, a resident of Laguna Beach, California, hit on the notion of hiding hash inside electronic equipment carried by touring pop groups. He lined up an accomplice in London to organize the racket. From a luxury flat in West London, a man called Morris began contacting managers of a number of pop groups. He said that he knew of a good manufacturer, the Cripple Creek Case Company, that specialized in making fiberglass baffles for the amplifiers used for electric guitars. Several pop groups agreed to let him supply the equipment. The new loudspeakers were sent to the United States by air freight ahead of the performers.

All went well on six occasions. Then a curious customs man at Kennedy Airport in New York took a look inside one loudspeaker cabinet—and found 25 kilos of hashish. A swift search of the 14 other amplifiers in the shipment—destined for a Las Vegas night club—revealed hash in the fiberglass baffles of each cabinet. In all there were 350 kilos worth several million dollars. In London the police rounded up the managers of three pop groups and the cabinet maker, but the alleged organizers, Morris and Combs, vanished overnight.

The hazard of smuggling through airports is always that a keen customs man, even without a tip-off, will catch a consign-

Above: regularly, the son of the Dutch Minister of Health reads out hashish prices over the radio. The leaf symbol he is wearing on his sleeve is the leaf of the marijuana plant— a familiar shape to the users.

ment sooner or later. A British doctor and his pretty accomplice thought they had a much safer plan. He fitted out a luxury 53-foot yacht, and set sail from England's west coast for a romantic voyage to the West Indies. During the voyage he and the woman made a secret stop to take aboard about 2000 kilos of marijuana worth nearly $1 million. The drug was neatly packaged in 47 waterproof bales. After lazing in the Caribbean sun for a while, they sailed northward to Canada. They rendezvoused in a lonely cove 25 miles south of St. John's, Newfoundland, where some accomplices waited on the cliffs. But an alert local fisherman got curious about the small rubber dinghy, laden with packages, being ferried back and forth from the yacht to the beach. He notified the police, who swiftly tracked the boat to a nearby harbor and arrested the doctor and his companion.

Such transatlantic enterprises, however, hardly match the avalanche of marijuana that pours over the border into the United States from Mexico. It comes by ship, plane, car, truck, and even in packages thrown over the chain link fence that guards much of the 2013-mile-long border. So much passes by in the moonlight every night it is a wonder that people living in towns like El Paso, Texas, or San Diego, California do not get turned on as it is spirited by. Step into the storage room for confiscated pot at the customs headquarters in San Diego and that is almost what happens. As much as 20 tons may be stacked there at any moment, and the powerful smell makes a visitor almost lightheaded. Once in a while the customs burn up a big

Below: the cannabis smuggler shows the same original flair as smugglers of other contraband. These plates were molded carefully out of hashish in India, painted, and then mailed to San Francisco, where they were seized by vigilant customs agents. Four arrests were made.

amount of confiscated pot—but in a furnace not in the open air. Otherwise half of Southern California might get high on the smoke.

All this pot comes from cannabis plants grown in the provinces of Chihuahua, Durango, and Zacatecas in the interior of Mexico. A host of amateur and professional operators from the United States trek down there to buy it, hoping to win themselves a slice of the $5-billion-a-year American retail market for marijuana. The amateurs mostly hide it in their cars, and the wiser ones have learned that two particular makes of car have ideal hiding places. They poke around the used car lots of Los Angeles or San Francisco in search of either an old Ford Thunderbird or a late 1950s Chevrolet. The Ford, often voted "car of the year" by smugglers, has two excellent hideouts, measuring 8 feet by 8 inches by 4 inches, under the back seat. The recommended Chevrolet has a neat compartment in the fender behind each headlight, which will easily hold 15 kilos of pot. Equipped with the right car the smuggler heads across the border into Mexico at the San Ysidro checkpoint just south of San Diego, and seeks out one of the well-known marijuana dealers in the boisterous town of Tijuana. Tijuana thrives on lively horse racing, cheap tequila, and an array of goods for smuggling ranging from pot to wrist watches.

No one makes much of a secret about it. The undercover men from the United States drug enforcement agencies who go into Tijuana incognito know who is doing most of the big selling—

Above: customs agents now have to learn more elaborate techniques than the rough-and-ready methods of the past. Here an instructor shows how to make an identification of opiates.

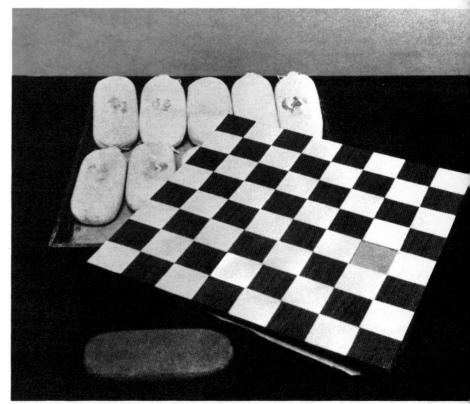

Right: this apparently innocuous chessboard concealed over a pound of hashish in its secret compartment. It was mailed from Israel to the United States, and seized in the customs investigation made in New York.

just as the dealers know who the agents are. One American agent used to delight in ringing up a leading marijuana dealer at 4 a.m. just to needle him. "I'm going to bust you Chico," he would say to the man he had roused, and then he would hang up. Occasionally an outraged dealer tries to get his own back. He will arrange for a little shoot-out as the agent comes through the border. But an agent with good contacts can usually rely on getting a tip-off. The shooting of a federal agent would create too much heat for all concerned, and be self-defeating. "But you can't be too careful," said an undercover agent, hauling a revolver out of the trunk of his car and putting it beneath his coat as he set off for a night in Tijuana.

Catching the big fish is almost impossible. The important dealers rely on mules, and know better than to try to send drugs through the ordinary border checkpoints in cars or trucks. They use the sea or air. Scores of private planes flit back and forth over the border, land in Mexico on lonely roads, stock up with drugs, and dodge back through the clouds to touch down at some remote airport in New Mexico or Texas.

Above: Mexico has long been an abundant source of supply for users in the States. This cache was detected in Detroit as the smugglers transferred it from a refrigerated truck to a pickup.

The $3 Million Pot Haul

One classic game of tag between customs and mules spanned the United States from Calexico, California to New Jersey. Customs agents, acting on a tip-off, picked up an old Ford station wagon as it came through from Mexico, and followed it discreetly. They had no idea whether it would lead them 100 miles or 1000. As it turned out it was over 3000. After one brief overnight stop in a motel to rest, the two men in the Ford turned east and drove steadily hour after hour from California into Utah and then Wyoming. They seemed to be heading for Chicago. They drove at a leisurely 45 or 50 miles an hour, obviously taking care not to be picked up for speeding. After a day and a half of driving nonstop except to buy gas, they reached Chicago. Other customs agents alerted by radio were waiting for them. But they didn't stop. They circled to the south of the Windy City, picked up the Ohio Turnpike, and got on the Pennsylvania Turnpike toward New York.

The nerves of the customs agents doing the tailing were on edge. They had to keep that Ford in sight without making the driver suspicious. On the turnpikes one customs car would trail for a while, then fall back or pass to let a second car sit behind the Ford. Finally, after 96 hours on the road the Ford left the New Jersey Turnpike and headed for a quiet street in suburban North Bergen, New Jersey. A cheerful Cuban came out to greet the two men, and opened his garage doors for them to drive inside. But the weary customs men pounced. Their catch was a major New York pot dealer, Angel Roberto Millan, and $300,000 worth of neatly packaged marijuana bricks inside the Ford they had followed all across the United States.

Their catch was a modest one when set against the all-time

record seizure. That was made aboard the *Don Miguel*, a sleazy little Mexican freighter. It had been towed into Los Angeles harbor by a tug one evening from its home port of Mazatlan, Mexico, and moored at Berth 187. The freighter had been rented to Universal Studios, which was going to use it for some waterfront scenes in an episode of the TV show *Ironside*. When the television policemen, led by actor Raymond Burr, turned up for filming the next morning, they found that the real police had been there before them. The boat was swarming with county detectives and special customs agents, who had been keeping the boat under surveillance by radar and patrol boat the whole way from Mexico. They had had a tip-off that the real profits of the *Don Miguel's* voyage to Los Angeles was not the rental fee paid by the film company. They went through the boat with dogs especially trained to sniff out drugs. Sure enough, down in the forward hold, the dogs became interested in a pile of wooden crates hidden under stacks of cartons. According to lettering on the crates they contained coffee, but the scent drifting out of them hardly had the coffee fragrance. A customs agent pried one crate open; inside were carefully packaged one-kilo bricks of marijuana. The agents then broke open all 384 cases in the consignment. There were 7000 bricks of pot in all—a haul of 7000 kilos worth nearly $3 million on the streets of California's cities and towns. The supply line to a major southern Californian dealer had been broken.

For customs it was a new record, a seizure to be proud of; but in terms of the pot coming into the United States, it was hardly worth mentioning. A haul of $3 million in a $5 billion traffic is no sign of winning. There is too much profit to be made on the rest that gets by.

Left: early in 1976 the 105-foot fishing trawler *Lillian B* was stopped by customs men off North Carolina. It contained 25 tons of marijuana from Colombia at a street value of $25 million—had it arrived.

The New Gold Rush

4

The dusty alleyway off one of the bustling streets of Dubai, a busy seaport at the southern end of the Persian Gulf, appears to lead nowhere. But halfway down on the left, an opening in a high white wall reveals a short flight of steps going up to a broad flat roof. On the far side a door opens into a cluttered room that is refreshingly cool after the oppressive outside heat of a July afternoon in 1974. Within are four men, all in open-necked white shirts and slacks. In one corner a telex machine is clattering, and two telephones on the desk rarely stop jangling.

Behind the desk a big man with a drooping black mustache cradles one phone over his right shoulder, the other over his left, and speaks alternately in English and Arabic. "Okay, what time? . . . Right . . . 1000 tolas . . . okay, usual payment." He hangs up and shouts something in Arabic into the other phone. Now another man puts down the bottle of Pepsi Cola that he has been drinking through a tattered straw, and goes over to a safe in the corner. He unlocks it to reveal a stack of neat fiberboard boxes. He breaks the metal sealing strips around one box and opens it. Inside are rows of neat little bars of pure gold, each no bigger than a matchbook. These he carefully counts out and puts into an attaché case. He stops at 100. That is the 1000 tolas ordered on the phone, for each of these luscious wafers weighs 10 tolas (3.75 troy ounces, the standard measure for gold). He snaps the briefcase shut, and goes out into the dusk with $65,000 in gold under his arm.

By Dubai standards that is nothing to get excited about, because Dubai has built itself a unique reputation as the world's greatest center for smuggled gold. In a good year as much as $500 million in gold passes through. For good measure, the smugglers handle another $50 to $100 million in silver as well. Not for nothing has Dubai been christened "the smugglers supermarket."

The port's trump card is that it happens to have the best safe haven for boats within easy striking distance of the shores of Iran, Pakistan, and India. The high-powered dhows that line Dubai's little creek can make the 2200 mile round-trip to Bombay quite comfortably in 10 days. The payload on the outward trip may be about $1 million in gold, while for the return

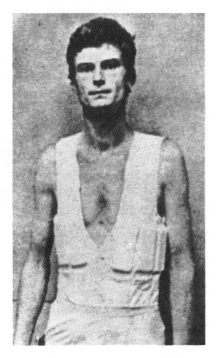

Above: an Austrian carpenter-turned-gold-smuggler with his golden vest, shown at Tokyo airport, where he was picked up with his undeclared riches.

Left: gold, the universal and eternal symbol of wealth and security. Here it is in the form of 10-tola bars, equivalent to 3.75 troy ounces in weight and to a small chocolate bar in size. The 10-tola bar is particularly popular in India, which is kept well supplied by the gold smugglers.

Above: the dhows of Dubai rock peacefully at the water's edge of the Persian gulf city, waiting for their cargos of gold bars that will be speeded off to meet the insatiable demand of gold-hungry India.

voyage the dhows load up with bars of silver that are smuggled out of India as part payment for the contraband gold coming in. Dubai's other ace in the smuggling game has long been that its ruler, Sheik Rashid Bin Said Al Maktoum, has displayed great commercial flair in transforming his small sandy domain into the Hong Kong of the Persian Gulf—a free port where all manners of goods from gold to diamonds, watches, or textiles can come and go without any complications like import duties. The smugglers operating out of Dubai, therefore, are acting perfectly legally until the moment that their boats steal inside the Indian or Pakistan 12-mile limit. In Dubai they are safe.

Dubai tends to attract the limelight. But for each ounce of gold aboard those boats stealing softly over the Arabian sea, there is usually another ounce passing along some other less well defined smuggling pipeline elsewhere in the world. France, Spain, Morocco, Italy, Brazil, Egypt, Turkey, Indonesia, Thailand, and many other nations are all potential honeypots for the gold smuggler. Only about 70 nations, among them Switzerland, Canada, the United States, Lebanon, and Singapore, allow their citizens to hold gold freely and do not prohibit its import. Another 150 nations either charge a high tariff on gold or ban its import altogether. They offer the gold smugglers a wide, nearly insatiable market. In some years, as much as half of all the world's newly mined gold passes along smuggling channels at some stage on the way to its final destination. That represents a total busi-

Above: because of currency restrictions the smugglers will not accept Indian rupees in exchange for their gold, and so it has to be paid for with hard foreign currency, or, often, with silver. These silver bars, smuggled out of India to pay for gold smuggled in, are loaded onto the waiting London-bound airplane. Below: street gold dealers with their trays of gold bars, openly on sale in Dubai. Possessing or selling gold is perfectly legal, and the dealers ask no questions about the eventual destination.

ness worth almost $2 billion, on which the profit may well have been close to $200 million—a return that would do credit to any multinational company. Gold smugglers have a good rule of thumb to determine whether or not a route is profitable: the difference between the free market price at which they can buy the metal openly in London or Zurich and the black market price in the country in which they eventually sell it must be at least $75 a kilo, or a little over $2 a troy ounce, to cover all expenses. Profit is added above this margin.

In making their profits, the smugglers' ingenuity knows no bounds. Gold is smuggled by air and by camel caravan. It may be cast into strange shapes and passed off as machine parts, tourist souvenirs, or ashtrays. It is known that some of the furniture shipped to the embassies of Arab sheikdoms in such countries as Pakistan has been dispatched with hollowed out table legs filled with gold. An official visit by a head of state from, say, a Middle East country to India may provide even better cover. The gold travels in the baggage of his entourage, which is never searched as the host country rolls out the red carpet to welcome its distinguished visitor.

A cunning ruse dreamed up in Ceylon—another source of illicit gold—was to fasten the lids of the boxes of families moving across to India with nails of pure gold. These were extracted and melted down into bars at the end of the journey. A trick devised to get gold into Japan was to hide it in the false bottoms of drums of motor oil being shipped from Vancouver, Canada to Tokyo. Certain models of Mercedes cars are smugglers' favorites because of a handy secret compartment behind the dashboard. Up to 50 one-kilo bars of gold can be hidden there, carefully wrapped in strips of black velvet to stop them from rattling around.

The gold game is very much for professionals. The amount of money tied up in a single illicit shipment is rarely less than $50,000, and is often more than $1 million. Consequently the smuggling has to be organized as efficiently as any business, and the financing must be carefully arranged. In fact, the only difference between a gold smuggling operation and much legitimate gold dealing is that at some crucial stage the smuggled gold has to pass through a port of entry into the country of destination, either an airport or harbor, without the formalities of customs declarations.

The gold smugglers have another distinct advantage: their operations do not attract the same kind of international police attention as those of the drug traffickers. They are, after all, only infringing customs regulations in the country for which the gold is destined; they are not breaking the laws of the country from which they actually operate. In fact there is no real secret who the big gold smugglers are; they are as well known to the authorities as to the gold-dealing fraternity. It is just that nothing can usually be pinned on them. For example, the Indian customs authorities and Revenue Intelligence Service have tried for years to get the British to do something about the sale of gold to Dubai. But they are told politely that such sales are perfectly legal.

The main safe havens from which the gold smuggling syndicates operate are Geneva, Brussels, Beirut, Hong Kong, Singapore, and, of course, Dubai. Vientiane, Laos was also a favorite jumping off point until 1975, when the Communist takeover there made further operations impractical. No matter where the smugglers work from, every group relies on buying its gold on one of the two great wholesale markets, London or Zurich. The strength of these two cities is simply that they handle the marketing of all gold from the world's two great producers, South Africa and the Soviet Union, which mine 85 percent of all gold.

The Handy Small Gold Bar

The South Africans and Soviets sell all their gold as "good delivery bars" each weighing 400 troy ounces and, with gold at $160 a troy ounce, costing $64,000 apiece. The London and Zurich markets thoughtfully reshape much of this gold into handy small bars to suit all pockets. Although the British and Swiss gold smelters are perfectly legitimate, they are fully aware of the illegal use to which most of their reshaped bars will go. The most popular bars for smuggling to France, Spain, Morocco, or Turkey are one-kilo bars, each the size of a half-pound bar of

Above: the rich gleam of gold in vaults in Johannesburg, South Africa. The Soviet Union and South Africa are the main gold-producing nations, between them mining 85 percent of the total world gold production.

Right: a Soviet gold bar with its stamp and serial number. These gold bars are shipped legally to Zurich and London, there to be reshaped to meet customers' requirements.

Above: one-kilo gold bars, the favored size for smuggling into France, Spain, Morocco, or Turkey, are stamped with their serial numbers in the bullion room of Johnson Matthey, London dealers.

chocolate, and costing about $5000. Ten-tola bars, or "biscuits" as they are nicknamed, worth about $600 each are the favorites in India and Pakistan, while a 10-ounce bar is most desirable in Malaysia. The type of bar required is a good guide to the ultimate destination of gold going to a smuggling center such as Beirut or Dubai. Beirut, for instance, usually orders kilo bars, because it is the chief supplier to Turkey. But if Beirut starts ordering 10-tola bars from London as well, it will mean that someone in the Lebanese city has a line open to India or Pakistan. Singapore is another regular customer for kilo bars, which are then spirited across the Java Sea to Indonesia, but this crossroads of the East also takes some ten-tola bars for casual customers, who want a few to take on ships bound for Madras, Calcutta, or Colombo.

The London gold dealers and the Swiss banks are not, of course, a party to the smuggling in any way. They are simply selling gold to legitimate clients such as commercial banks and authorized gold dealers. They are not concerned with what happens to the gold once it has been paid for. To the eventual customer, however, the true origin of the gold is important because there is a constant danger of fake bars that have been filled with lead or cement. So even at the far end of the smug-

69

gling pipeline, perhaps in some remote gold market in Bandung, Indonesia or Lahore, Pakistan, the local gold dealer will insist on seeing the approved stamp of a recognized London or Swiss refiner. The most widely known bars are those made by Johnson Matthey of London, and they are readily accepted all over the world. There can hardly be a gold dealer anywhere who is not familiar with the Johnson Matthey stamp. New European refineries find it hard to break into this small bar business, because no one is familiar with their stamp, or "chop," and a man buying from a smuggler in Borneo can hardly check its authenticity in Switzerland. The only place where London or Swiss bars are not always preferred is in the Far East, where most smugglers move either the one-tael (1.33 troy ounces) bars of two leading Hong Kong dealers, King Fook and Choi Tai Fook, or thin wafers bearing the chop "Kim Tranh; Saigon, Hong Kong, Hanoi, Phnom Penh."

Gold-lined Vests

Whatever the preferred bar, the simplest and quickest way to smuggle it is by air, except for such short hauls as from Geneva into France. Then road travel is much more practical. Several major syndicates have long specialized in shifting tons of gold by using couriers flying scheduled airline routes. The technique is entirely straightforward. Beneath his shirt, the mule wears a tailor-made canvas jacket with pockets into which kilo bars can be slotted. A strong courier can quickly learn to carry between 30 and 40 kilos at a time, although a little training is essential. The first time anyone wears a 30- to 40-kilo golden jacket he is likely to fall flat on his face the moment he bends over.

One syndicate, which was operated for a while from London by a graduate of Eton, carefully put together its own training manual. It laid down that every courier must wear a belt or suspenders, put in new shoelaces, and carry a needle and thread, safety pin, and buttons. This first aid kit was vital to prevent exposing his hidden load in case he popped a shirt button en route. The fresh shoelaces reduced the chances of one breaking, which he could not bend over to fix. Each mule also took a pack of pep pills for greater stamina. They were also advised, "Always dress English, with collar and tie. Avoid casual gear. At airports nobody gets stopped unless they draw attention to themselves. Be polite and relaxed with officials, but never humble." This syndicate recruited most of its couriers through advertisements in the Personal Column of *The Times* of London, mentioning rewarding trips to faraway places. The boss once revealed that he got the most replies from bored salespeople at Harrods, a prestige London department store. They were taken with the idea of a trip to Bangkok or Djakarta with all expenses paid as a pleasant change from facing haughty customers.

Two other key syndicates working out of Geneva relied mainly on mules recruited from the West German cities of Cologne,

Dusseldorf, and Frankfurt. In each of these cities they maintained a recruiting officer who lined up likely prospects. Taxi drivers were particularly keen on the job as a welcome relief from traffic jams. After being well briefed in advance, they went to Geneva or Brussels to pick up their golden loads. In Brussels a member of the syndicate usually treated them to a night on the town. The basic fee was $200 plus all expenses. In addition, if they were unfortunate enough to get caught the syndicate undertook to look after their families while they were in prison. That happened rarely, because things had often been arranged with customs. It was one of these syndicates that gave all couriers a club tie as identification, and also as a sign to any accomplice in customs not to search the wearer thoroughly.

Despite all precautions, however, crises occur. One man became so terrified, for example, that instead of getting off the plane as instructed in Bangkok, he went on to Hong Kong. For a few hectic hours the syndicate office in Geneva thought he had absconded with $50,000 in gold, and sent someone around to see if his wife knew where he was. But he turned up in Hong Kong with the gold still safe and sound, and someone else took it to Bangkok.

Smuggling by gold-jacketed couriers became so widespread for a while that it was often a question of guessing which of the passengers on flights to the Far East was not a courier. A leading smuggler once admitted that on a flight from Hong Kong to Tokyo one day he was the only passenger without gold, and that all the others on the plane were mules for him—unbeknownst to them.

This classic method of gold smuggling has had a severe setback in the 1970s because of increased airline security against hijacking. Body searches at an airport inevitably reveal any gold bars on a person. Although it may not be illegal to carry gold, there is always a danger that the authorities at the departure airport will tip off colleagues at the mules' destination. This happened to two couriers who were picking up gold from the Caribbean island of Curaçao, which is a handy jumping off point for South America. When the spate of hijacking to Cuba was at its height, searches were introduced in Curaçao, and the two mules bound for Argentina were found with gold corsets. This was not illegal in Curaçao, but it was a different story in Argentina. They were promptly arrested when they got to Buenos Aires. A message to customs had arrived ahead of them.

The changing pattern in gold smuggling has been to establish jumping-off points much closer to the eventual destination. In this way much of the smuggling has become short-haul, and can be handled by surface transportation. Beirut, for instance, once the launching pad for literally hundreds of mules a week bound for such far-flung cities as Tokyo, Djakarta, or Bangkok, now concentrates on its near neighbors Turkey, Syria, and Egypt. And Dubai, as we have seen already, has become the staging post for India and Pakistan.

Above: some gold smugglers don't manage to make a delivery. Here a Seattle customs officer takes the one-kilo bars out of a smuggling vest and records their serial numbers. The unfortunate courier had been picked up at Seattle airport.

The demand for gold on the Indian subcontinent is closely interwoven with its social and economic traditions. Gold is as important to the Indian as an American Express card and a life insurance policy is to an American. The village farmer who has a good harvest puts the profits into gold jewelery, which he keeps as insurance against a bad monsoon or some other disaster. The concept of savings accounts or investments is totally unknown to him. As for paying taxes—well, as everywhere, the more of his wealth he can hide, the less he pays. Tons of smuggled gold are concealed as untaxed wealth. But at the heart of the Indian passion for gold is the custom of exchanging gold at marriage. The bangles and bracelets with which the bride is endowed become a walking life insurance policy, and gold exchanged becomes a measurement of the prestige of the two families being united in marriage. Ten to 15 tolas (over five troy ounces) is an ordinary offering—an enormous amount compared to western wedding rings, which may contain perhaps one-eighth of a troy ounce. This custom explains why India has been a sponge for precious metals for centuries. Since 1947, however, the import of gold has been forbidden, and the only way it can come in is by the back door.

Gold for India

Dubai has shrewdly capitalized on the Indian demand. A fleet of custom-built dhows regularly plies between the Arab seaport and the west coast of India. Each is equipped with a 320-horsepower diesel engine giving them a burst of speed that leaves customs launches standing. In preparation for the outward voyage, the 10-tola gold bars are carefully slotted into pouches in canvas jackets. One hundred bars, weighing about 10 kilos (22 pounds) go into one jacket, and a shipment will often be described simply as 20, 30, or 50 jackets.

While the dhows are at sea, carefully worded cables go to confederates in Bombay. One night some five days later Indian fishing boats slip out to sea to meet the Dubai dhows. Ten or 15 miles offshore, they pull alongside in the dark and a swift transfer of jackets takes place. The Dubai boat then turns for home or runs down the coast for a second rendezvous with other boats laden with bars of silver. The silver is smuggled out of India in part-payment for the gold, and also to sell elsewhere because the international price for silver has generally been higher than the Indian domestic price for several years.

After the pickup the fishing boat comes ashore with the gold, usually at a small village not far from Bombay. The jackets are thrown onto the beach where a regular unloading team is waiting to distribute them. They rush the gold to Bombay by car, which is parked at a prearranged place and left. A few minutes later someone with a spare key makes the pickup. He leaves the gold in an empty apartment that the syndicate has rented temporarily, and other carriers come there to pick up one or two jackets at a

Above: Kirkran Kourlian, a Jordanian picked up at Tokyo airport in possession of nearly $70,000 worth of gold bars. Japan has an increasing demand for gold, most of which is made into fine jewelry. There are more affluent Japanese wanting to buy gold jewelry than the domestic gold production can keep up with, and so the smugglers helpfully bridge the gap.

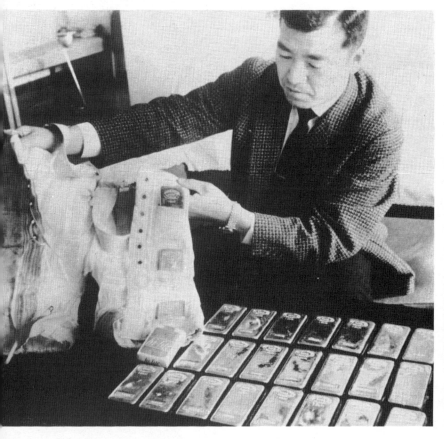

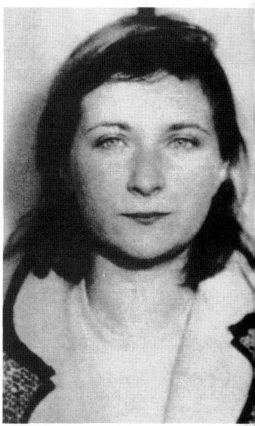

time. Each man usually receives one rupee (13 cents) for every
tola he moves, and $130 for a jacket. Security is maintained at
each step by keeping participants ignorant of each other. The
fishermen do not know the unloading gang, the car driver does
not know the pickup man, and the mules only know an apartment. Having worked only by signals, no one can identify
anyone else.

Trying to combat gold smuggling into India has proved an
almost insuperable job. The Indian customs authorities lack the
money and equipment to match the smuggling syndicates.
Besides, a customs officer who turns his back or goes for a stroll
at the right moment can earn perhaps a whole month's pay. The
smugglers also have friends in high places who have often been
able to thwart any serious attempt to break up a syndicate.
Officials who are too conscientious may find themselves moved
to less desirable posts. Once a particularly dedicated senior
official of the Revenue Intelligence Service managed to successfully infiltrate the smuggling groups. He made so many seizures
of gold that for a few months the traffic almost stopped. Then he
was shifted to an obscure inland city. Business boomed again.

A more determined effort was made to stop the smuggling in
1974. Many of the leading Indian smugglers were simply thrown
in prison without trial, and held for more than six months. The
traffic slowed down when these bosses, who had previously
seemed immune from punishment, suddenly ended up in jail

Left: the crew of a smuggling dhow making the gold run to the coast of India from Dubai. The skippers of the dhows are paid handsomely enough to minimize the temptation simply to disappear with the cargo, and the odd one who tries usually pays promptly with his life.

Below: even the most reliable dhow run from Dubai to India does on occasion go wrong. Karachi customs officers here display gold bars that were dumped by a gang of smugglers, and recovered from the mud by the long arm of the law.

overnight. But even that breathing space was only temporary.

While India has been soaking up gold for centuries, markets like Vientiane, Laos may flourish just for a few years to cope with some special local crisis. Vientiane, a steamy town on the banks of the Mekong River just across the border from Thailand, is also handy for Burma and South Vietnam. It suddenly became a gold smuggling center in the mid-1960s to meet the craze for gold generated by the war in South Vietnam. Most of the action was in the hands of the local branch of the Bank of Indochina and three or four Chinese merchants on the town's one main street. They bought gold from Swiss banks and sold it to all comers, usually for cash over the counter. It was a delightfully informal business. The gold kilo bars came by air from London or Zurich to Bangkok, Thailand. There the boxes of gold were transferred to local flights of Thai Airways or Royal Air Lao for

the 400 mile hop to Vientiane. Frequently the gold was just tucked under the passenger seats of ancient DC4s that Royal Air Lao operated. On arrival at Vientiane's Wattay Airport, the boxes of bullion were swiftly unloaded, often directly into the trunk of the car of the local Bank of Indochina manager. If demand was brisk, he dispensed it almost as casually as candy bars to his eager customers outside the customs shed.

Most of it in fact was being swiftly spirited to Saigon. Often Royal Laotian or South Vietnamese military aircraft on goodwill missions between the two countries took along a couple of hundred kilos. Everyone was in on the racket. One Laotian prince, off on a visit to Paris, insisted on first going to Saigon in an official plane to deliver 500 kilos of gold. Since gold brought $150 more per kilo in Saigon than in Vientiane, he made $75,000.

In Laos, payment for the gold was often in American dollars

that were the profits of other black market operations inside South Vietnam. The bills were smuggled from South Vietnam through the little town of Pakse on the Laos–South Vietnam border. The favorite subterfuge was to wrap the dollar bills in polythene bags and conceal them in five-gallon drums of fish sauce, a regular Vietnamese export. All this money ended up in the Bank of Indochina in Vientiane, which often smelled more like a fish market than a bank.

Vientiane's Heyday

Three-quarters of the smuggled gold went to Saigon, and most of the rest to Bangkok. One enterprising former French foreign legion man living in the Thai capital set up a nice gold business. He made the round-trip by road to Vientiane twice a week, bringing back 50 kilos of gold each time. On this he made a tidy profit of $5000 a week. Naturally he became a familiar figure to Thai customs officials at the little border town of Nong Khai, and he was on friendly terms with most of them. They knew him simply as a traveler who came through on business regularly. Familiarity nearly ruined his racket, however. One day one of the customs men asked the Frenchman to take him and his family back to Bangkok. Even though the Frenchman had his usual 50 kilos of gold already hidden in the car, he had to say "yes." Soon after they set out on the bumpy road south, the Frenchman heard a distinct clink of gold bars. One or two of them had slipped out of the velvet in which he always wrapped them individually. He thought quickly. "Let's have some music," he said, turning on the radio full volume. He kept the radio blasting for the entire 10-hour journey.

Vientiane's gold days came to an end with the winding down of the Vietnam war. With the American withdrawal the vast black market profits were no longer being made, and the bar girls of Saigon—who had put much of their earnings into gold—lost their GI customers. If anything the smuggling went into reverse. There was a mad scramble to get money out of South Vietnam, and also Cambodia, before the final Communist takeover of both countries. During 1974 and 1975 Vientiane started selling back to Europe almost as much gold as it had bought during its heyday. The gold, mostly in the form of melted down bangles, trickled in to Vientiane from all over Southeast Asia as people cashed in their gold to keep it out of Communist hands. In the final dash to leave in the spring of 1975 the only things thousands of refugees took with them were the waferlike Kim Tranh bars.

While Vientiane gold smuggling flourished because of war, Singapore developed an equally profitable traffic because of the wild inflation in neighboring Indonesia. Business with Indonesia was so brisk that some banks in Singapore even set aside special changing rooms in which the smugglers could put on their jackets filled with gold. To confuse anyone trying to tail them, the mules usually arrived in groups of three or four, each bringing along a spare shirt. (No one wears a jacket in Singapore because it is too hot.) Inside the bank they all changed to the second shirt, and then left simultaneously by separate exits, making it virtually impossible for a tail outside to identify and follow all of them.

Not all gold smuggling is so far-flung. One of the best customers for Geneva gold dealers is France, which is practically just up the road. Although the French have the reputation of being Europe's greatest hoarders, with gold tucked under their beds and buried in their gardens, the legal import of the metal into the country is strictly controlled. In theory the gold that is traded on the Paris Bourse every day comes from a seemingly unlimited pool already within the country. In fact it is recently arrived bullion spirited over the border by the ton from Switzerland. The business is highly organized and "accidents" are rare.

One summer's day in 1975, for instance, French customs men stopped a car at the border near Geneva. After much searching, they found a hideout under the back seat in which nestled just over $1 million in kilo bars. The compartment was concealed with a care worthy of James Bond. It could be opened only by performing these five distinct operations in the right sequence: (1) remove the clock from its mount; (2) disconnect two electric wires behind it; (3) put the gear shift lever into reverse; (4) lift the back seat up and swing it forward behind the front seats; (5) switch the headlights on. Investigations revealed that this secret compartment had been used for over a year to ferry millions of dollars of gold into France.

Britain has also become a target for gold smugglers, although London boasts one of the world's great gold markets. This is because its gold is strictly for export. The ordinary British citizen is not allowed to hold gold bullion privately. He may, however, own gold coins. During 1974 and 1975 the declining fortunes of sterling turned many Britons into gold coin buyers for the first time. The favorite was the South African Krugerrand coin, containing precisely one troy ounce of gold. For a time these coins could be freely imported and sold openly by London dealers. But the rush for gold met with stern disapproval from the government. In April 1975 the import of Krugerrand coins, also called Krugers, was banned.

Within weeks a premium of over 20 percent developed on the Krugers already in the country. Each became worth about $35 more in Britain than just across the Channel in Belgium, West Germany, or Switzerland. Not surprisingly, a brisk undercover trade soon developed. Customs, however, moved equally swiftly. Within a matter of weeks of the ban on imports, customs officials had ferreted out almost $1 million worth of Krugers. By applying the customs men's rule of thumb that they are lucky to catch more than five or 10 percent of illicit goods, the implications are that perhaps as much as $10 or $20 million worth of the coins slipped safely through—yielding someone a profit of between $2 million and $4 million in just a couple of months.

Undercover Diamonds
5

Above: a fortune in brilliant diamonds, glittering in the diamond merchant's scoop. Immensely valuable, small, and universally desired, they are an ideal line of goods for the smuggler—once he manages to get his hands on the gems. Left: in some places, finding the diamonds is easy. This woman lives in Koidu, a bush town in Sierra Leone in the middle of the diamond area, where diamonds are scattered in the gravel all around. The inhabitants have developed a way of walking with one eye on the ground: the Koidu crouch.

The scene—the tropical west coast of Africa.

It is just before midnight and the moon is not yet up. The only flicker of light in the steaming African night is the endless sparkling of the fireflies. The only sound is the chirrup of insects. An old white Mercedes lurches down a muddy road and halts beside a tall clump of trees on the fringe of a swamp. Now two other sounds can be heard—the clank of pickaxes and the scrape of shovels digging in gravel. A tall man in a thick silk shirt leaves the Mercedes and makes his way through the trees toward the diggers. A half dozen of them are gathered around a shallow pit. They barely take notice of the stranger's arrival. One of the diggers—a big man armed with a long stick and a knife stuck in his belt—detaches himself from the group and comes over to the visitor. They exchange a few words quietly. Then the new

arrival turns, walks back to his car, and speaks to his companion. "He says they are just turning the gravel over now." As he puts the car into gear and bounces off down the road, he explains, "they'll be back at first light to see what stones they've turned up. They'll come around to the house with anything tomorrow evening." By "anything" he means diamonds.

Nocturnal diamond digging is commonplace around Koidu, a raucous little town tucked away in the bush of Sierra Leone, because this is the heartland of one of the world's richest diamond fields. Diamonds are scattered like so much stardust in, around, and even underneath Koidu Town. Anyone forking over a vegetable patch has a fair chance of coming upon a gemstone of value, even one of four or five carats. Strictly speaking, of course, all these diamonds belong to the government of Sierra Leone or, more properly, to the government-controlled Diamond Mining Company that has an exclusive concession on several hundred square miles of gravel swampland around Koidu. Most people living and working in and around the town find that the diamond company's wages can hardly compare with the fat rewards offered by the unofficial diamond dealers who, like the man in the Mercedes, haunt Koidu. These dealers in their turn hardly want to pay the 7.5 percent export tax the government imposes on stones shipped out legally, even if they could explain how they got them in the first place. So many, perhaps most, of the diamonds of Koidu are smuggled out of Sierra Leone to the diamond markets of Europe.

Policing the area is largely a waste of time and effort. As one leading diamond buyer put it: "I could hide a whole regiment in the elephant grass up there." Anyway the *dash* (bribes) paid by the illicit dealers can usually insure that the diamond company's night watchmen are conveniently looking for maurauders in one area of the swamp while a "night dig" is going on in another. No one really knows the full extent of illicit diamond mining, known as IDM, in Sierra Leone. But even government officials concede that at least half of the country's diamonds are illegally mined and smuggled out—a traffic worth over $50 million a year.

IDM is the established way of life in Koidu and other diamond mining villages nearby, so much so that everyone goes around in a kind of lurching walk known as the Koidu crouch, with one eye constantly cocked at the ground in case they stumble on a diamond. While nights are the busiest time for IDM, especially

in the main fields, the illicit digging goes on openly by day in the bush around Koidu. A bird's-eye view from a helicopter operated by the diamond company's security force reveals hundreds of Africans scattered through the bush, as if on some vast picnic. Let a helicopter come into view over the cotton trees and they flee for cover, leaving a trail of spades and buckets behind them. The security police, however, can do very little. The moment their helicopter vanishes over the horizon, the diggers are back again. New security men often start out with the best of intentions, but soon get caught up by temptation when bribes start coming in from arrested smugglers. Cash payments of $5000 and $10,000 convert the zealous rooky policemen to a philosophy of live and let live. "The trouble is corruption," says a police chief sadly.

Ease of Diamond Smuggling

Disposing of the choice rough diamonds presents the diggers with no problem. In the evenings they make their way to the home of one or another of a handful of Lebanese dealers with headquarters in Koidu. The entrance halls look rather like a dentist's waiting room with all kinds of people sitting around waiting for their turn in the inner sanctum. Over cups of sweet black coffee, the dealer looks at the stones on offer. This stage is christened IDB—illicit diamond buying. If he likes what he sees the haggling starts. An agreement may be reached quickly, but if the diamond digger is not satisfied he may go to another dealer. If a deal is arranged, the broker pulls out a thick wad of bills from his safe and carefully counts out the price. In the course of an evening he may pay out $5000, $10,000, or $50,000 in cash. There is not much argument over these stones, most of which are only one or two carats in size. Occasionally, however, a digger turns up a real prize—a diamond of 25, 50, or even 100 carats. Then the gossip quickly spreads among the dealers, and each sets out to get his hands on the walnut-sized blue-white gem for as little as possible. Every dealer has his network of spies and informants, and is ready to offer a little dash here and there at all times. The rewards for a good tip-off are handsome.

The next step in IDB is for the dealer to smuggle his stones out of the country, for which the diamond is the smuggler's best friend. As Ian Fleming, the creator of James Bond, once observed, "You can carry enough diamonds on your naked body to set you up for life." A good operator can conceal two or three small diamonds in his mouth, tucked behind his back molars, and still carry on a normal conversation. Diamonds packed in a rubber condom can safely be carried internally. Women, as it is often pointed out in smuggling circles, are twice as well endowed for this as men.

In fact, nothing so elaborate or uncomfortable is required to spirit illegally mined diamonds out of Sierra Leone. The dealers themselves jump into their cars—Mercedes preferred—and

Left: in Sierra Leone the official National Diamond Mining Company maintains its own security force to police the fields. Here illicit diamond miners flee from the police helicopter hovering overhead.

Below: a security team catches and arrests an illegal miner, with his equipment as evidence.

speed off over unpaved roads through the bush on the 500-mile round trip from the Koidu fields to the border of Liberia. Smaller independent operators simply hail a taxi in Koidu and haggle over the price to the border. The cost, depending on one's bargaining skill, is about $250. The easiest crossing point is at Melema, a tiny village on the Moa River, which marks the border. There a friendly boatman will ferry anyone across to Liberia, by-passing the customs checkpoint on the way. The obliging taxi drivers from Koidu will even wait a day or two until the smuggler returns. Once the smuggler is across the river, he either locates another taxi or is picked up by a friendly dealer who has driven down from Liberia's capital, Monrovia. A few of the better organized operators flit back and forth in their private aircraft, landing and taking off from jungle clearings.

Whatever the route, any seller can be sure to find eager buyers waiting for him, either in Monrovia's Ducor Palace Hotel or in one of the all-night bars. In Monrovia—the Mecca of IDB—

Above: selling the rough diamonds. Dealers with their
headquarters in the diamond
country see an endless stream
of diggers, each with his
precious stones to sell.

Right: the De Beers buying
office in Sierra Leone. Many
of the diggers go straight to
the one main legitimate source
of diamonds to the world's
dealers, the De Beers Central
Selling Organization. It
operates its own buying offices
in direct competition with the
illegal diamond dealers, often
offering higher prices in the
attempt to drive them out.

leading dealers who come from Europe to take full advantage of Sierra Leone's illicit diamond mining think nothing of buying up $250,000 worth of rough diamonds at a time. The fact that Liberia annually exports 10 times as many diamonds as it produces never seems to bother anyone. "I may handle $2 million of rough diamonds a month," admitted one buyer, "and perhaps only 20 percent of them are actually found in Liberia. The rest come from Sierra Leone. I reckon to have 50 visitors from there on a good day."

While the only real trick in smuggling diamonds from Sierra Leone is to have a large roll of bills from which to dispense liberal amounts of dash, the filching of stones from the famous diamond coast of Southwest Africa (Namibia) is a genuine challenge to any man's ingenuity. This diamond "desert" is a narrow strip of sand dunes 300 miles long and about 10 miles wide between the Namib Desert and the Atlantic Ocean. Since the Europeans first began the despoliation of Africa, this arid coast has been a hazard to sailors and an obstacle to overland travelers. But for the lure of diamonds probably no one would willingly go there. The lure is compelling, however. Beneath the dunes the gravel is peppered with the finest gem diamonds in the world. Every year up to $200 million worth are turned up.

The only inhabitants of this region are Europeans and Ovambo tribesmen working for Consolidated Diamond Mines (CDM), a privately owned company that maintains this mining area as one of the most closely guarded private estates in the world. All staff members, both European and African, live there for long periods. As workers and executives come and go, they are subject to most rigorous scrutiny. Most furniture, once in, is never allowed to leave. All personal articles from books to baby rattles must be x-rayed before being allowed to leave. But diamonds are still smuggled out.

It is as if the very tightness of the security and the close confines within which everyone lives creates an almost compulsive need to try to beat the system. Getting hold of a diamond is not really hard. After the sand dunes are bulldozed, every nook and cranny of the diamond-bearing rock below is picked over by hand and then swept with brooms. During these operations sharp-eyed Ovambo tribesmen who work in the diamond fields can often pick up and secrete a diamond on their bodies. The challenge is not to find a gem, but to get it out of the area.

Over the years all kinds of legends of success and failure have grown up. One man is said to have worked there for years building up a little cache of diamonds. His plan was to orbit them over the boundary fence in a homemade rocket. Unfortunately his rocket blew up on the launch pad. Another would-be smuggler left his stolen diamonds behind, planning to pick them up a few weeks later by landing on the beach in a private plane. He found his diamonds, but as he tried to take off, the nose wheel of his plane got stuck in the sand. One European worker hid some diamonds in chewing gum just before he checked out of the company compound for the weekend. When the security men called him in for his routine check, he managed to stick the chewing gum under the rim of the table in their office. He was searched, found to be clean, and allowed to go home. The next time he went on leave, he purposely picked a fight with the security man on duty after he had been searched, complaining that he was always being harrassed. As he shouted, he peeled the old chewing gum from under the table and slipped it into his mouth. But an alert guard noticed him and he had to give up his gum and his diamonds.

Stealing Is Only Half the Game

The prize goes to the man who conceived the idea of concealing the stones inside the bolts of his car. He took the bolts out of the engine mount and cut through them well down toward the thread end. He drilled out the inside of each bolt and packed it with diamonds. He then welded the two sections together, put the bolts back in place, and screwed the nut over the hairline crack of the join. He got away with his cache, but was caught trying to sell the diamonds to a South African dealer.

Stealing diamonds in the desert or from mines in South Africa is only half the game. The other half is disposing of them, and this can only be done through illicit buyers. They in turn either smuggle them out to Europe or try to get them "legitimized" in South Africa itself so that they can be exported legally. One way to make stolen diamonds appear legal is to pass them off as part of the normal production of the alluvial diamond diggings around Kimberley, the scene of the first diamond rush to South Africa a century ago. In the Kimberley area, a few of the old-timers who still work independent claims may be persuaded to "salt" their claims with illegal diamonds from the coast or inland mines. The South African police maintain a Diamond Detective Division in Kimberley, one of whose jobs is to spot such doings. When a new diamond mine producing distinctive green-hued diamonds opened in Finsch a few years ago, the detectives in Kimberley swiftly noted that similarly colored diamonds suddenly began to be found in local diggings. The illicit buyers had placed their agents in the new mine, and had routed their haul through the ancient diggings.

Working all angles, the diamond detectives also try to trap illegal buyers by undercover agents who offer a nice haul of diamonds—from a special police stock, of course. The agent spins some long story about how he spirited the stones out of the mine he works in, and the mine officials provide cover for him. He tries to persuade the dealer to buy. Occasionally the trap can be sprung, but buyers are notoriously wise to the ways of police. "We are lucky if we recover 10 percent of the IDM we even *know* about," said one detective.

Sooner or later most diamonds, legal or illegal, find their way into the tight-knit and exclusive fraternity of international

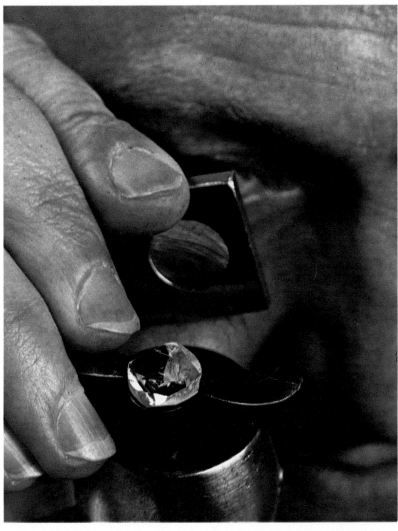

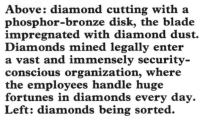

Above: diamond cutting with a phosphor-bronze disk, the blade impregnated with diamond dust. Diamonds mined legally enter a vast and immensely security-conscious organization, where the employees handle huge fortunes in diamonds every day. Left: diamonds being sorted.

Above: the finished cut gem being inspected for any flaws. Whether it was originally mined officially and passed through the system, or whether it was found by an illicit digger or smuggled through some stages in its progress, it will almost certainly pass into the hands of the De Beers firm, which markets over 80 percent of the world's new diamonds.

diamond dealers operating from Antwerp, New York, Paris, Tel Aviv, Vienna, or Milan. They take care of the skilled cutting and polishing that must be done to make rough stones gleam seductively for the eventual buyer. Perhaps the world's finest diamond cutters are those in Antwerp and Tel Aviv. So, diamonds stolen on the diamond coast, in Sierra Leone, or in Zaire, Angola, and Ghana (the other hotbeds of IDM) generally pass into the mainstream of the diamond business in one or the other of the two cities.

Most of the world's diamond dealers get their fresh supply of diamonds from one main legitimate source, the De Beers Central Selling Organization. Central Selling markets over 80 percent of the world's new diamonds, including not only those from De Beers' own mines in South and Southwest Africa (Namibia), but also from Sierra Leone, Zaire, and Botswana. It runs buying offices in these three countries. Central Selling operates alongside the unofficial buyers in Monrovia and other centers of IDB. If a new supply route for smuggled rough diamonds opens up, Central Selling—which runs its own extremely efficient intelligence network—will swiftly set up shop to buy them in direct competition with the illicit dealers. The De Beers buyers will often try to force IDB dealers out of business by offering better prices. That is, for a while. The priority from Central Selling's point of view is to get as many diamonds as possible. The organization's basic philosophy is simple: by controlling the marketing of most of the world's new diamonds, it can maintain the world price in an orderly fashion.

Central Selling filters its diamonds out to dealers at 10 sales a year: 250 dealers receive a personal invitation to each sale, known as a "sight." An invited dealer advises Central Selling in advance of the approximate value of diamonds required, but the firm determines the precise mix in the packet he gets. Although the dealer can question the price for the packet, he must take all or nothing.

The dealer who does not get his supplies at a sight may buy from other producers who sell direct—or from the smugglers. African operators usually deal through special contacts in Europe, to whom they deliver openly. Occasionally, however, they delight in cloak-and-dagger games. A leading Antwerp dealer once took the train to Paris to appraise a parcel of smuggled diamonds. He was met at the station, blindfolded, and driven by a roundabout route for half an hour to a large building. There he was guided upstairs into a blacked-out apartment. The diamonds were laid out on a table for him to view. He appraised them, agreed on a price, and slipped them into the rolled-up black leather pouch in which all dealers carry their stones. He was then blindfolded again for the return journey to his hotel. Everything was done with great courtesy, but he had no idea where he had been to buy the smuggled diamonds.

Where Is Mr. Big?

Such security is hardly needed nowadays because there is not much pressure on the diamond smugglers once they get the gems to Europe. Some years ago, however, Sir Ernest Oppenheimer, chairman of De Beers, decided to set up his own international diamond police force to break the IDM and IDB networks operating out of Africa. He hired Sir Percy Sillitoe, former head of British secret service, to ferret out the diamond smuggling syndicates. Sillitoe launched into the game with great gusto, and created a far-flung International Diamond Security Organization (IDSO) having a network of undercover operatives in Africa and Europe.

The IDSO operatives, provided with lavish funds, tried all kinds of maneuvers. They could be found in bars and shady hotels in all the countries of southern Africa, trying to buy illicit diamonds and to build up a picture of the whole IDM–IDB racket. Some of the undercover agents soon became convinced that somewhere there was a "Mr. Big" in control. Although they did succeed in contacting a few sellers of stolen diamonds,

Above: Sir Percy Sillitoe, the former British secret service chief who undertook the job of bringing into existence the International Diamond Security Organization. It was set up to eliminate illegal diamond mining and dealing in Africa.

Right: one of the Central Selling clients inspects his "sight" of diamonds. He gets this opportunity to buy 10 times a year, and he is given a parcel of diamonds offered at a fixed price. The rule is that he must take all or none.

Above: this cartoon published at the time of ISDO's organization is supposed to be of Sir Percy in disguise. There was a great deal of publicity about the ISDO from reporters enchanted with the prospect of cloak and dagger stories, though secrecy was important.

Mr. Big—if he existed at all—remained elusive then as now.

Half the problems of Sillitoe's globe-trotting diamond detectives was that they were surrounded by a blaze of publicity, which is hardly the best thing for an undercover operation. Before long, De Beers decided it would be prudent to disband Sillitoe's detective agency. Since then the company has operated its diamond intelligence on a much more discreet but highly effective level, based on better liaison with regular police forces through Interpol.

For every rough diamond smuggled out of Africa, a cut and polished stone is being smuggled into India or Japan, Italy or the United States for an eventual buyer. The motive for smuggling may be to avoid import duties or to hide illegal profits without paying tax on them. It isn't only dewy-eyed girls about to get engaged who have taken to heart the De Beers advertising slogan that "A diamond is forever." Many a Mafia boss realized long ago that diamonds—discreet, readily convertible to cash, and relatively inflation-proof—provide a secure way of putting aside some of his take. In India, which has a tradition of hoarding gold, diamonds have come increasingly into favor as restrictions on holding gold have been tightened.

"Most of the diamonds I sell are smuggled, because it saves so much in taxes," admitted a handsome young Italian gem salesman as he zoomed his Mercedes 275SL down the super highway from Milan to Bologna. "I have a Polish girl friend, a

countess, who brings them over for me from Switzerland. She carries them inside her, if you understand? The ladies are very good at smuggling like that. But it does have to be someone you can trust."

Trust, in fact, is all important in any part of the diamond business. Any deal is sealed with a handshake and—whether the dealer is Jewish or not—with the Hebrew blessing *mazel broche* (good luck and blessing). Such trust also shields the small number of unscrupulous dealers who handle illicit stones in what the trade politely calls "the parallel market." Their fellow dealers are not going to ask questions as to how they came by the diamonds; nor are they going to answer questions from police or customs men investigating smuggling. "I didn't know what silence was until I went to Antwerp to ask about some stolen diamonds," one investigator said ruefully.

The Little-known Hub
Such silence cloaks the fact that Antwerp is the heart of the diamond business. The action centers on Pelikanstraat (the street of the Pelican). It is a narrow street of three- and four-story buildings near the main railroad station. It seems to be inhabited only by dealers in their black homburg hats hurrying back and forth between their offices and the exclusive Antwerp Diamond Club where they pull out the stout black leather pouches, roll diamonds onto the table, and start to do business.

If he wants to smuggle his stones to a client in the United States or Japan, the dealer will be extremely cautious. After all one can hardly trust the stones to an unknown mule, who may be a criminal. So most diamond smuggling is done by friends or reliable friends of friends. The simplest way of all is to entrust them to the postman. The diamonds are taped to a piece of cardboard and sent first class airmail as ordinary business papers without a customs declaration. In 99 cases out of 100 they will reach their destination without a customs check. There are slip-ups, though. According to one story, for example, the United States customs officers in New York were once showing the Customs Commissioner, up from Washington, how they sorted through airmail from abroad. "Now, sir," said an eager agent, picking out a buff envelope, "we are pretty sure this one contains pornographic pictures." He slit it open. Inside were $10,000 in diamonds neatly stuck to two thin pieces of cardboard.

A dealer from Antwerp worked a neat twist for smuggling diamonds into the United States. He went to New York by ship, and during the voyage hid a cache of diamonds in his cabin. When the ship docked he walked through customs openly with nothing to declare or fear. Another member of the gang reserved the same cabin for the return voyage scheduled a few days later. Yet a third member came aboard for a small party to wish him bon voyage, as friends often do. The diamonds were swiftly

Above: at a quiet table, a dealer in the Pelikaanstraat, Antwerp—where most of the diamonds eventually are sold—evaluates another gem for sale.

removed from their hiding place, and when the "all ashore" bell sounded, the friend walked off the ship with them.

A dealer who plans to smuggle stones into the United States without the trouble or risk of thinking up his own scheme can usually make contact with a professional diamond smuggling team. A New York dealer, for instance, having bought $200,000 of diamonds in Antwerp may want not only to avoid the import duty into the United States, but also to dodge the income tax on the profit he will make from the sale of the stones. In a small bar close to Pelikanstraat he meets a member of a smuggling team. Together they go to an independent appraiser, who values the diamonds. The smuggler then agrees to deliver them to the dealer in New York within, say four days, for five percent of their value. He accepts all risks, and guarantees restitution in case the diamonds are stolen or, as is more likely, the smuggler is caught by customs. In effect, the dealer's shipment is insured. He himself flies home and awaits a telephone call telling him precisely where and when he can pick up his diamonds. The beauty of this system is that the dealer does not know how the smuggling is done, and cannot be a liability if something goes wrong. And he gets his money back in the unlikely event of his stones being seized. The very fact that the smugglers can "insure" the diamonds indicates that seizures are rare.

The smuggling of diamonds through customs can be done in myriad ways. The mule may carry the gems internally, or secrete them in a tube of shaving cream or toothpaste. Hollowed out shoe heels are another favorite hiding place. All are known to the customs agents. However, they may have been fooled in the macabre tale of a girl who lost an eye in a car accident, and took to smuggling diamonds in the cavity behind her glass eye. The likelihood of a smuggler being subjected to a thorough search is remote, because most customs men nowadays are looking for the mule with heroin taped around his body or hidden in his suitcase. Since the heat has switched to drugs, the diamond courier has little to worry about. He can feel even more confident because most arrests are made on the basis of tip-offs, and telling tales is rare within the close-knit diamond fraternity.

Right: the smuggler (on the right) and his shoes. Leiser Weitman tried to get 250 industrial diamonds through United States customs, concealed in his hollowed-out shoe heels. The authorities show how it worked.

Variations on a Theme

No one is totally immune, however, especially if they draw unnecessary attention to themselves. Not long ago a senior pilot with a major international airline took to smuggling diamonds regularly to finance a somewhat expensive affair he was having with a German air hostess. The fact that he was supporting his family in a nice home, and also living it up all over the globe with his girl friend aroused the curiosity of the airline's own security chief. One day the security chief took the pilot, a good friend, quietly aside, and said, "I don't know exactly what you are doing to pay for it all, but take my advice and stop it now." The infatuated pilot took no notice of the warning, and a couple of weeks later landed with still another consignment of diamonds from Antwerp in his pocket. As he handed them over to his contact at the airport—a baggage loader—the customs men nabbed him. His career, as well as his affair, was ruined.

Diamond smugglers often rely on the fact that a customs man cannot possibly be an expert gemologist, and simply outwit him. The easiest way is for a dealer to send a package of stones openly by registered airmail complete with customs declaration. But inside he will have comingled a wide variety of stones, some good, some poor, some large, some small. The true value of the shipment might be $150,000, but he values it at $95,000. The customs man who looks at the package will amost certainly accept the valuation. The dealer not only has saved himself duty on $55,000, but also can save the tax on the sale of the stones not officially on his books.

A variation on this theme has been used for years in Manila, capital of the Philippines. Filipinos have long preferred diamonds to the gold jewelry so desired in most other places in the Far East; but the Philippine government has levied a high tax on the import of precious stones. Tax-free diamonds, however,

Below: a Cuban refugee, Luis Hernandez-Noa, smuggled his wealth out with him by forcing two diamonds in his front teeth. The human body seems to have plenty of places in which a stray diamond—or even more—can be discreetly concealed.

are available in Hong Kong only two hours away by plane. So the wealthy Filipino woman who wants a few new diamonds just boards the plane to Hong Kong. As she leaves Manila she declares that she is taking out with her a fine necklace set with diamonds, and gets a permit to bring it back in. What the customs official does not know is that the diamonds on the necklace are fakes. When she gets to Hong Kong the woman goes to her friendly diamond dealer, and replaces the fakes with genuine diamonds. She then flies home, waves her permit to the customs officer, and gets her diamonds in duty-free.

For most people such trickery is only a good game. Dodging the duty on diamonds is not the same as smuggling heroin. In fact, for some it becomes almost a compulsion. Consider the case of Charles Travitsky. He was arrested in Miami on the way home from Venezuela carrying $47,330 worth of diamonds internally in contraceptives. While out on bail, he was again arrested in Miami as he flew in from Brazil with diamonds sewn into the seams of his suit. A few months later he again got out on bail, and was promptly nabbed in Mexico with $12,000 worth of diamonds. Next it was the turn of the Thai Customs. Acting on a tip-off they searched Travitsky's luggage when he landed in Bangkok from Singapore. Sure enough, he had diamonds, rubies, and sapphires hidden inside a portable record player and in cans of fruit salad. Apparently he just could not resist smuggling.

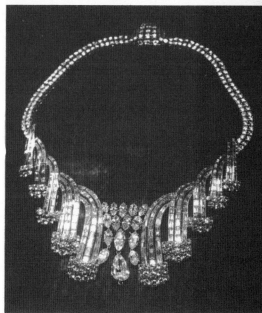

Above: more than loose stones are smuggled. This dazzling diamond necklace is a spectacular prize seized by the United States customs officials.

93

Trafficking in Treasure
6

What does an illicit dealer in Stone Age artifacts do when he believes he holds a treasure of historic importance and wants to hawk it discreetly to the highest bidder on the international art market? The problem is much greater than for other smuggled goods that must be authenticated. Gold can be assayed, heroin can be quickly tasted on the tip of the tongue, diamonds can be scrutinized with a loup. The knowledgeable seller and the sophisticated buyer can usually be sure that the goods offered are what they claim to be. When it comes to smuggled art and antiquities, however, the carefully woven net of intrigue surrounding their authentication may itself seem like an intricately constructed work of art.

The extraordinary affair of the Royal Treasure of Dorak makes this point clear. The story begins in Turkey.

Archeologist James Mellaart had just settled back into his seat on the train from Istanbul to Izmir. Comfortable—and gazing idly at the activity in the station as the train got underway— he scarcely glanced at the young girl who came into his compartment and settled in the seat directly opposite. Although the girl made little impression, Mellaart's eye was quickly drawn to the bracelet she was wearing. It appeared to be of solid gold worked in a design that had been found only in the ancient city of Troy. No archeologist could resist such bait. James Mellaart, then assistant director of the British Institute of Archeology in Ankara, leaned forward and introduced himself, explained his interest, and asked the young woman where the bracelet came from. From her home, she said innocently. It was part of a collection of antiquities that she had in her home in Izmir. Mellaart found it easy to get himself invited to see the collection —and to dinner.

After leaving Izmir station together, Mellaart paid little attention to where they were going. They took a taxi to the pier, crossed the bay by ferry, and then took another taxi through a warren of narrow streets to a simple house. All the time, Mellaart talked nonstop to the girl, who spoke English with an American accent. She introduced herself as Anna Papastrati. Over dinner she began to describe and place before him the rest of the collection. Mellaart did his best to conceal his excitement

94

Above: James Mellaart, the distinguished British archaeologist. He became embroiled in the mysterious affair of the royal treasure of Dorak, apparently stolen from an ancient tomb by a smuggling gang.

Above: Kazim Direk street, the place where Mellaart says he was taken by an elusive girl. Since 1958, when Mellaart met her, the street name and house numbers have all changed.

Right: one of the Dorak daggers shown in a Mellaart drawing.

as he looked at gold and silver figurines, bracelets, daggers, and drinking cups of pure gold. If Anna's claims were true, the treasure had been buried in two royal tombs about 4500 years ago. Here, it seemed, was a unique archeological find. Cautiously he asked if he might examine the whole treasure, and perhaps have it photographed. The girl hesitated, and then said that she did not want outsiders to know about the treasure. Instead she suggested that Mellaart stay with her several days, sketch the objects, and take all notes he liked.

Mellaart took her up on the offer, and stayed in the house in Izmir, drawing and taking rubbings of all the objects. Anna explained that they had been excavated from tombs near the

village of Dorak south of the sea of Marmara, which had been a center of a culture that had flourished in a state neighboring ancient Troy. Mellaart worked without a break, never leaving the house. If he needed anything Anna shopped for him. Before he left, Anna promised that she would shortly send photographs of the objects to him. Mellaart had been so obsessed with the treasure that when he left the house, the only facts he knew were Anna's name—at least the one she had given him—and her address.

Mellaart never set eyes on Anna or her treasure again. For some months he kept quiet about his adventure and waited for the photographs that never came. All he got was a whimsical letter from Anna authorizing him to publish his sketches. It was then that Mellaart took the drawings and his story to Professor Seton Lloyd, the director of the British Institute of Archeology in Ankara. Lloyd exclaimed that they were dynamite. On his next trip to London, Seton Lloyd and other eminent British colleagues arranged for their publication in the archeological pages of the *Illustrated London News*. This long-established periodical has an international reputation for reporting only bona fide archeological finds.

From the moment of publication of "The Royal Treasure of Dorak," Mellaart was surrounded by a controversy that nearly marked the finish to his distinguished career. The Turkish authorities, who forbid the removal of any work of art from Turkey, jumped to the conclusion that Mellaart had illegally excavated and exported a national treasure comparable to that of Tuthankhamen. Neither Anna Papastrati, the treasure, nor the house in Izmir could be traced. There were some who insisted that Mellaart had invented the whole thing.

There is, however, another explanation. Possibly James

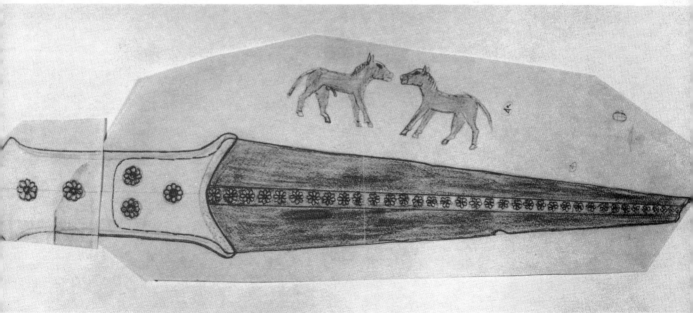

A GODDESS AND HER HANDMAIDENS—IN UNIQUE FIGURINES OF 4500 YEARS AGO.

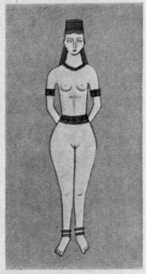
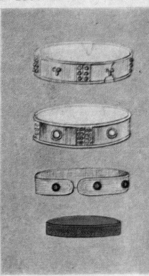

FIG. 3. THE TWO BRONZE FIGURINES—PRIESTESSES OR WORSHIPPERS—WEARING WHAT WAS PRESUMABLY THE NORMAL DRESS OF THE YORTAN RULING CLASS (6 INS. HIGH).

FIG. 4. BACK VIEW OF FIG. 3. THE FIGURES ARE OF BRONZE WITH SILVER GARMENTS; AND HAIR, ORNAMENTS AND DECORATION IN GOLD. TWO HAIRSTYLES ARE SHOWN.

FIG. 5. ONE OF THE ATTENDANTS ON THE GODDESS. THE BODY IS ENTIRELY MADE OF SILVER, THE HAIR AND ALL THE ORNAMENTS BEING GOLD.

FIG. 6. PERSONAL JEWELLERY FROM THE QUEEN'S TOMB: GOLD AND SILVER BRACELETS, WHOSE PATTERN MAY ALSO BE OBSERVED ON THE FIGURINES.

FIG. 7. THE GODDESS (RIGHT) IN ELECTRUM AND HER PRINCIPAL ATTENDANT IN SILVER, ALL THE ADDITIONAL ORNAMENTS BEING IN GOLD. THE GODDESS'S GOLD BELT AND PENDANTS ARE SOLDERED ON BUT THE "GRASS SKIRT" IS ENGRAVED. LIFE SIZE.

FIG. 8. THE BACK VIEW OF THE TWO FIGURINES SHOWN IN FIG. 7. THE SILVER FIGURE, WEARING A GOLD-EDGED SILVER APRON, HOLDS A CIRCLET, WITH SEVERAL BIRDS ON IT—PERHAPS A MUSICAL INSTRUMENT OF THE SISTRUM TYPE.

It is not absolutely certain that these five amazing figurines in electrum, silver and bronze were actually found in the two tombs; and Mr. Mellaart, while convinced of their genuineness, thinks that they may be a little later. All are about 6 ins. high, cast in a two-piece mould and are naturalistic though a little flat. All the articles of dress, hair, necklaces, bracelets and anklets were made in sheet gold or wire and were added by soldering or sweating-on, or, in some cases, loosely fixed. It is noteworthy that the objects of jewellery are exactly to be paralleled among the jewellery found with the queen in the double tomb; and Fig. 6 shows a group of bracelets from that tomb—two of them were found round the queen's arms—which exactly resemble the bracelets worn by the figurines. There seems little doubt that the electrum figure represents the goddess, the two silver figures her close attendants and the bronze figures her priestesses or worshippers. The silver figurine in Fig. 8 is especially interesting. It is suggested that the rod in the left hand was used to beat the bird-studded circlet in the right hand to produce a musical note. One of the bronze figures holds a similar circlet.

Left: a page from the *Illustrated ted London News* article that Mellaart wrote about the Dorak treasure, with his illustrations of many of the remarkable finds.

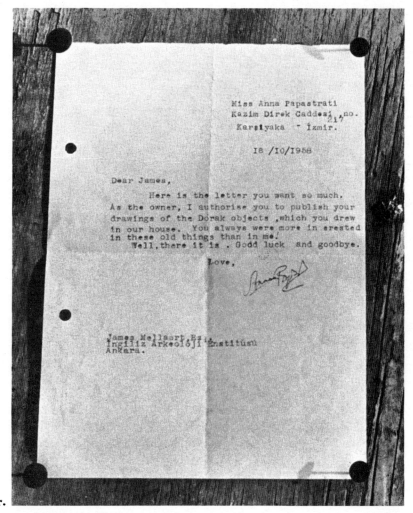

Right: Anna Papastrati's typed letter giving Mellaart her permission to publish his work on the Dorak treasure. Since that letter, Mellaart says he has heard nothing more from her.

Mellaart had been the innocent victim of a clever group of illicit art dealers. It now seems possible that the treasure of Dorak had been discovered and illegally removed from its site by a smuggling gang, but could not be offered to the type of collector who could appreciate it and afford it at a price anywhere near its true value until some unimpeachable authority had authenticated it. What better way to achieve this than to have the treasure scrutinized by a well-known and qualified British archeologist, and to have the story of the find appear in the *Illustrated London News*? In archeological circles there is a rumor, based more on prejudice than fact, that the Dorak treasure now sits in the basement of an important American museum.

That works of art should travel in the same undercover way, if not along the same routes, as diamonds, gold, and heroin, is one of the more amazing new developments in the world of contemporary smuggling. The smugglers who walk through customs with a valuable painting rolled up inside an overnight bag, or an ancient gold drinking cup wrapped in pajamas in a suitcase, play these games partly out of bravado. An American smuggler specializing in Mexican antiquities confessed: "You must not

Above: the Euphronios Vase at the Metropolitan Museum of Art in New York. It is agreed by all that it is a superb example of a Greek vase, but the route by which it arrived in New York is a matter of considerably greater controversy. The Italian authorities insist it was excavated by Etruscan tomb robbers and smuggled out of the country. The museum officials are just as adament about their story of an absolutely legal purchase from a family that had owned the vase for over 60 years.

forget one thing. I am a pirate, I enjoy piracy. I like the moment at the airport when they look at my passport and glance at my bag, for I take the best pieces with me, on the plane.''

This smuggler and others like him also peddle a good line in self-justification. It goes like this: dealers in smuggled art are really performing a public service. As they sometimes like to say, they do nothing more than rescue works of art by finding them comfortable resting places and owners who will value them highly. But like all smugglers, the thing that keeps them in the business is the money. Vast sums now change hands in the international art market.

Every newly independent country wants to signal its arrival on the world scene by establishing an airline, a soccer team of international caliber, and a museum. At the same time, many private collectors pursue their genuine enthusiasm for early or contemporary works of art, while other collectors view paintings, sculpture, fine furniture, and antiquities as investments that may be more secure than stocks and bonds. Today works of art seem to hold their value even in times of inflation.

If collectors regard art objects as part of international currency, so do dealers, smugglers—and thieves. The art boom has produced a complementary rise in the extent of the looting and pillaging of art and antiquities from ancient sites. It was plunder rather than military action that recently stripped the temples of Bangladesh. It is organized looting that results in the nearly daily announcements of the disappearance of some important work from a church or museum. Many of the countries in which known works of art are plentiful—and in which unknown and undiscovered works are also known to exist in plenty—have tried to protect their national heritage by forbidding or severely controlling the export of all works of art. The traffic in objects of Greek, Egyptian, Mexican, or Italian origin has not, however, been stopped. It has merely been driven underground.

Collectors as Receivers

The days of "finders keepers," when a man like Lord Elgin could simply walk up to the Parthenon in Athens and ship home to Britain some of its most choice marble sculptures, have gone forever. How then are private collectors and museums to acquire new items? Often the illicit dealer is the only one who knows. Even when works of art appear in the plush salesrooms of London or New York, the auctioneers cannot always be sure who the previous owner was. Private collectors ask few questions about the origin of art they are offered by sellers, provided that the object is authentic. One California millionaire who has paid some of the highest prices for European paintings in the auction rooms also collects Asian sculpture. He candidly admits, "I spent between $15 and $16 million in two years on Asian art, and hell yes, most of it was smuggled."

Even museums and public galleries, while forced to denounce the smuggler officially, turn out in practice to be remarkably understanding and tolerant of the method by which some objects that would enhance their collections arrive at the museum door. To save the director's face, some illicit dealers pay impoverished members of the European aristocracy to sign papers guaranteeing that a certain picture, tapestry, or vase has been in their family for the last 200 years.

A great sir was caused, for instance, when the Metropolitan Museum of Art in New York City announced that it had acquired for the sum of $1 million "the finest Greek vase there is," a hitherto unknown large *kalyx crater* (a cup or vase in which wine was diluted with water before being served to guests). The vase is the work of two great Athenian artists, the potter Euxithios and the painter Euphronios. The official press release from the Metropolitan Museum described the new treasure as having been in the collection of an old European family since before World War I, and declared that the wish of the previous owner to remain anonymous must be respected because he could be the source of future acquisitions.

A few months later, however, the Rome correspondent of the *New York Times* cabled an entirely different story to his paper. The expensive pot, he claimed, had been sold to the Metropolitan by Robert E. Hecht Jr., an American living in Rome. Hecht was alleged to have had a history of legal difficulties with the Italian authorities concerning irregularities in the export of works of art. The *New York Times* reported that art experts in Europe were of the opinion that such a magnificent vase could not have been entirely unknown unless it had recently been dug

Above: the rarely photographed Robert E. Hecht, who sold the Euphronios Vase to the museum. Italian authorities claim he has had a long history of legal difficulties with regard to the exportation of works of art. He claims it was legally acquired.

up. The suggestion was that the vase had been found the year before in an illegal excavation and looting of an Etruscan tomb. The Italian police asked the Americans to give their side of the story, and immediately issued a warrant for the arrest of Robert Hecht. It was admitted that Hecht had taken the vase to Zurich, Switzerland, where the American museum officials had first inspected it, and also that Hecht had flown to New York with the crated vase on the seat beside him. As the Metropolitan's spokesman proudly related, "Euphronios went first class." Despite the controversy and criticism leveled against it, the museum defended the original story, even expanding the details slightly in naming the previous owner as Dikran A. Sarrafian, an Armenian living in Beirut who was selling his treasures before emigrating to Australia.

Looting Etruscan tombs is an old Italian occupation—it has been going on since Roman times. North of Rome in the hills surrounding Cerveteri, the *tombaroli* (tomb robbers) work with cautious but consistent effort. One of their favorite methods of concealment is to build a shabby hut over a site on which they think a tomb is located, and leave it to molder for months until it becomes an accepted feature of the landscape. They then work inside it, breaking open the tombs and taking the treasure. So rich and complex was the Etruscan civilization, which flourished

2500 years ago, that their dead were buried in elaborate rooms. In these rooms, decorated to look like the earthly homes of the occupants, exquisite vases, statuettes, jewelery, and gold ornaments frequently surrounded the dead. The Etruscans themselves were assiduous collectors, and from their tombs most of the great Greek vases have been recovered.

Whether or not the Euphronios cup was, as the Italians claim, recently excavated, the Metropolitan had paid a record price to find itself the focus of international criticism. The most museum officials have conceded is to say that "if we were wrong, this is one of the most fantastic swindles that has ever been perpetrated."

At least the Metropolitan had the vase. Such compensation was denied to the Boston Museum of Fine Arts, which was forced to return to Italy a hitherto unknown painting by the Italian Renaissance master Raphael. The museum had acquired the small painting for a sum in excess of half a million dollars. An eminent art historian claimed that the painting, a portrait of an Italian noblewoman of the 16th century, was "unquestionably a Raphael." It was an exciting acquisition, and the museum at first basked in the interest it aroused. The public was informed that the picture had formerly been in an "old European private collection."

Among the people whose interest was caught by the picture was Rodolfo Siviero, Chief of Italy's Commission for the Recovery of Works of Art. Siviero was fascinated by photographs of the painting, especially by its frame. According to historical sources, such a portrait had been done by Raphael but the frame

Below: a group of antiquities plundered from Etruscan tombs near Viterbo, and since recovered. One Italian archaeologist reported that of 550 chamber tombs he discovered, nearly 400 had been previously stripped by the tomb robbers.

103

had been lost. The frame, thought Siviero, must be modern. Whoever had supplied the frame may also have had a hand in smuggling the painting out of the country.

Siviero began his search by talking to friends and contacts among the art dealers of Florence. He was led step-by-step to Ferrucio Ildebrando Bossi, a dealer living near Genoa.

Next, Siviero and the Italian police searched hotel registers in the Genoa area. They found that three officials of the Boston Museum had stayed in the city for several days some six months before. Under police questioning, Bossi admitted that he had sold the Raphael and its frame to the Boston art institution. Once Siviero began to make official accusations that the Raphael had been illegally exported from Italy, the museum was forced to acknowledge that it had imported the painting into the United States without making any kind of customs declaration. The picture had traveled in a museum official's suitcase. The laws of both nations had been violated. To make matters worse, a number of dealers began to question the authenticity of the work, and to suggest that the painting was heavily restored. One London dealer even insisted that it was "demonstrably a fake." The Assistant Secretary of the United States Treasury responsible for customs had little difficulty in persuading the museum that the painting should return to Italy. There remained one final irritation for the officials of the Boston Museum. It seemed extremely unlikely that they would ever get their money back.

Above: proud officials of the Boston Museum of Fine Arts with a stunning acquisition—an apparently unknown portrait by Renaissance master Raphael. Above right: a detail from the portrait. It was later conceded that the painting, even if by Raphael, had been overpainted.

Before the investigation was finished, Signor Bossi had died.

The perpetual questions "is it real?" and "is it worth the price?" plague the world of smuggled art. Dealers and collectors alike hope that the only one to be cheated is customs. There is seldom total agreement about any work of art, even in the open and reputable world of the international salesrooms and public galleries. Therefore in the undercover world of dealers whose wares come from who knows where, genuine works can often be regarded with deep suspicion. The case of the Maya mask, recounted in *The Plundered Past* by Karl Meyer, illustrates how vulnerable the smuggled art object is to rejection and, as a result, to possible loss and destruction.

The Mysterious Mayan Mask

Meyer tells how Dr. Josue Saenz, a discerning and respected collector of pre-Columbian art, received a phone call at his Mexico City home. The caller, who would not give his name, said: "I will have good news for you in two weeks," and hung up. Two weeks later another phone call urged Dr. Saenz to take the early flight the next day to Villahermosa in the south of Mexico. Saenz had built up his great collection over the years through his willingness to take unconventional risks. He appreciated the adventure of unpredictable discoveries, and had let it be known that he would pay the highest prices for works of art of the first

Left: Rodolfo Siviero, head of Italy's Commission for the Recovery of Works of Art. He saw the Boston Raphael and succeeded in locating the dealer who had sold it—a man with a police record back to 1924. Siviero managed to get the portrait returned to Italy.

Left: some of the Aztec and Mayan art objects that were seized in illegal transit by the Mexican government during only three months in 1972.

Below: Norton Simon, a rich California collector who prefers Impressionist and Post-impressionist art and artifacts of Asia. In 1972 he openly said, "I spent between $15 million and $16 million over the last two years on Asian art, and most of it was smuggled."

quality. Was he on the verge of another unique acquisition?

To find out Saenz boarded the plane to Villahermosa the next day. At the airport he was met by two rough-looking characters and taken to a single-engine plane that was waiting nearby. After takeoff, the pilot made a point of covering the compass so that Saenz would not know where he was being taken. The plane finally bumped down onto a newly cleared strip in the jungle. A group of peasants came forward to meet Saenz. No introductions were made. Instead, one of the group merely indicated smilingly that they had something to show to Saenz. They handed him a small mosaic mask encrusted with jadeite. It had a striking mouth full of filed human teeth and two animal fangs.

Saenz studied the object and decided that it was almost certainly a Maya mask—one of only a handful in existence. He asked to take the mask back to Mexico City for an expert's verdict, but the peasants insisted that he make a decision on the spot. When Saenz offered them around $2000, the peasant spokesman laughed, reached into his pocket to take out a recent Parke-Bernet catalog, and pointed to some of the prices at which pre-Columbian art was then selling. After some negotiating, Saenz wrote out a post-dated check for a much larger sum. He calculated that he would have time to get the mask examined, and if it turned out to be a fake, to stop payment on his check.

The authority on Mexican art who first looked at the mask suggested that it might prove to be a fake. Saenz tried to stop payment on his check, but found that it had already cleared. Annoyed, Saenz turned the mask over to a dealer and asked him to get what he could for it as a doubtful work. Within weeks it was sold to a North American dealer for the full sum Saenz had paid, and was smuggled out of Mexico, which prohibits the export of pre-Columbian art, into New York. There it was shown to Dr. Gordon Ekholm at the American Museum of Natural History.

Below: a bronze Shiva that had been stolen from a village temple in India. Simon paid a reported $1 million for it.

Although Ekholm disapproves of the smuggling trade, he likes to see anything that arrives from Latin America in order to keep track of important items. Ekholm examined the object under a microscope. He noticed that the mask appeared to have little pockmarks over the lower jaw, which suggested that a beard had once been attached to it. He knew that other authentic masks have the same kind of pockmarks. Ekholm thought it most unlikely that a faker would have known to include such a detail. He pronounced the mask to be genuine. Shortly afterward, rescued by Ekholm's sharp eyes, the mask was bought by the Bliss Collection in Washington where it is now displayed. Had it not been smuggled into New York, the mask might have been forgotten and eventually lost.

While the routes by which some paintings and art objects arrive in respectable museums and galleries may sometimes be mysterious, the road to a number of private collections can be criminal. The enormous greed for works of art, the colossal post-war boom in art prices, and the lack of any kind of international inventory of works of art, means that art theft frequently precedes art smuggling. Unscrupulous dealers, and on occasion collectors as well, may not only accept smuggled items, but also directly order items to be stolen. The huge upsurge in art thefts has disturbed the art rich countries, and has caused every major western European nation to form an art theft squad as part of its police force. These squads cooperate through Interpol. Unlike most police, the art theft squads work less to apprehend the thieves than to trace the stolen art and restore it to the original owners. The job is not easy. We live in a time when increasing numbers of criminals realize that accredited works of art are a reliable form of currency, easily transportable and disposable in

The Stolen Treasures of Urbino

All Italy was outraged at the theft on February 6, 1975. Three priceless Renaissance masterpieces gone! Three paintings of national and international importance stolen! How had it happened? Where had they been taken? Would they ever be recovered by the nation?

It was highly significant that the three stolen paintings—which were *The Mute* by Raphael, and *The Flagellation of Christ* and *The Madonna of Senigallia* by Piero della Francesca—were the finest works in the entire collection on view. This indicated that the thieves knew exactly what they were after, wasting no time on lesser works. Because such well-known paintings can hardly be sold on the open market, it also pointed to the possibility that the burglars were part of an art smuggling ring—and that they had lined up in advance a wealthy private buyer who would not show the paintings in public.

The theft occurred at the Ducal Palace in Urbino, a city in central Italy. It was not too surprising that entry to the Palace museum had been gained without great difficulty. Everyone knew how poor the security was in the Palace, there being only two guards for 40 rooms at night. Two broken panes in the window of the Sala degli Angeli, in which the Raphael and the Pieros were hung, showed how the entry may have been made. Everyone knew that the scaffolding left in the garden for over a year after some restoration work had been finished could help any agile thieves a good part of the way up the palace walls for entry through a window. Dr Rodolfo Siviero, head of the Italian Commission for the Recovery of Works of Art, said that the paintings had been stolen between the checks of the night watchmen, made only every two hours.

The outcry soon died down, but the patient and unpublicized search of the police went on. Their effort was rewarded 13 months later when, in March of 1976, the paintings were recovered. They were found in an ordinary hotel in Locarno, Switzerland, which is in the mountain lake region near Italy, after a raid by a party of Italian and Swiss police.

How the police knew to make the swoop at that place and time is their secret. In spite of fears that *The Flagellation* would have deteriorated beyond saving, it and the other two paintings were in no greater disrepair than would be expected under the circumstances.

Was Locarno really meant to be the final destination of the stolen paintings? It is doubtful. Experts at the time of the theft had insisted that the destination must be outside of Italy. They had also expressed doubts that the paintings would ever appear for sale on the commercial market—a hint that smugglers were involved.

Geneva was often mentioned as the destination because it is a well-known center for the sale of art treasures, however obtained.

Speculation ran rife. One newspaper report said that an international gang of Italian, French and Swiss smugglers had carried out the theft on the orders of a "mad millionaire." The ruthless collector, it said, was willing to pay a fortune in order to secretly own and enjoy the masterpieces.

If the paintings were supposed to be smuggled out of Italy, as so many of that country's treasures are, why were they found in Locarno? The mystery remains. But meantime, the three highly regarded paintings are home again.

Left: *The Madonna of Senigallia* by Piero della Francesca, one of the world-famous works of art stolen in 1975 from the Ducal Palace in Urbino, Italy.

Below: *The Mute* by Raphael was also taken from Urbino Palace.

Left: **Piero's** *The Flagellation of Christ*, **third of the stolen masterpieces. The condition of this painting was so fragile that authorities feared for its survival on being moved.**

Right: **the Muralto Hotel in Locarno, Switzerland, in which the police recovered all three treasures of the Urbino Palace.**

a world of monetary restrictions and instability. In addition, the psychological barriers that once protected a church or a museum no longer seem to deter anyone.

In 1974, 3500 paintings were stolen in France alone. Art thieves robbed or attempted to rob 67 museums, 131 chateaux, 212 churches, and 130,000 private homes. In Italy, the number-one target for all art thefts, officials refer to the "apocalyptic destruction" of their national heritage. In Italian police headquarters there is a large red book showing page after page of stolen and illegally smuggled works of art. A number of entries bear the word "recovered." But many do not. On a conservative estimate, more than $40 million worth of art is either stolen or illegally exported from Italy each year. Most of the smuggled art goes through Switzerland.

In London, art thefts are now running at around $100,000 a month. Throughout Britain, many burglaries display a selectivity that betrays either a scholarly accomplice somewhere in the background, or a knowledgeable dealer who has earmarked each painting or piece of silver to be removed. Scotland Yard's Art and Antiques Squad enlists the help of specialized journals, and when available, publishes photographs of recently stolen works as a guide to prospective buyers. In the *Art and Antiques Weekly*, a regular column entitled "Too Hot to Handle" lists and illustrates stolen works. From time to time a weekly television program flashes pictures of the latest stolen items on the screen. American police estimate that the total value of recorded art thefts all over the world is around $1 billion annually—about the same as the total value of legal international art deals.

The Art Smuggler's High Road

Most stolen art objects are easily transportable, and so make a handy package for the smuggler. The smugglers' high road out of Italy into Switzerland is protected by highly paid receivers, carriers, and corrupt officials. The vaults of some Swiss banks are allegedly full of stolen or illegally exported objects that the banks are prepared to accept as security on loans. To recover stolen art, the police depend on it being recognized by an eagle-eyed customs officer, being abandoned once the thieves realize how hot their property is, or themselves infiltrating a smuggling ring. In 1973 Italian police posed as art smugglers to trace and recover a $2 million Tiepolo painting, which had been stolen from an Italian church guarded only by an 84-year-old priest.

Many major paintings stolen from Italian churches and small local museums, which usually have one or two great works by the town's most famous sons, are so well known that they should be easily recognized by police and art dealers. To keep everyone's memory fresh, Interpol regularly publishes an illustrated poster of the ten most wanted works of art. Nonetheless some of the most famous pictures stolen in the last 10 years—like Titian's *Portrait of Pope Paul III* in 1971—are never seen again. It is suspected that they lie in the vault of a Swiss bank until such time as the search for them becomes less intense, or a *statute of limitations* (a law defining the period after which no legal action can be taken) comes into effect. With many less well-known paintings, silver, and furniture, there is little chance of recovery unless the owners have had the items photographed. Otherwise, how are police to alert customs and dealers to look out for a 17th-century Dutch seascape among the thousands that exist?

The apparent ease with which anyone can travel with a work of art was illustrated recently. The London *Daily Mirror* dispatched a reporter to Belgium with a full-size reproduction of a stolen painting at the time its theft was making headlines. The reporter made the journey twice, once by air and once by sea and rail, without anyone paying the slightest attention to him.

Another smuggling ploy is to put the name of some minor artist on a genuine work by a master. Is every customs officer to know the difference? It is thought that in Italy clever smugglers have paintings copied, return the copy to the owner, and export the original as a copy, with a suitably uninteresting customs certificate. Italian heirs to art collections sometimes abet this trade because it is the only way they can get around government restrictions in order to sell their inheritance to eager foreign buyers.

In the operations of the illicit art market, an unsuspecting tourist may be taken aside and offered a work of art at what is obviously below the market value. The usual story is that some local family needs to sell to raise money in a hurry. It is well to remember that the only reason for dropping the price on any work of art today is if that item is hot. Yet even those with the closest knowledge of art affairs can sometimes be taken in. Here is a case in point.

In recent years the opening of a new Paris gallery was somewhat clouded when it was discovered that one of the paintings in its opening exhibit, *La Femme à la Tête de Rose* by Salvador Dali, had been stolen from a Swiss gallery some three years before and smuggled into France. When the police informed the gallery owner of this, she was astonished. She pointed out that the painting had been lent for the show by Dali himself. How could it be stolen? The answer was that Dali had also been duped. He told police how the painting had recently come back into his own hands. The artist had been sitting in the bar of the Crillon Hotel one night when a man approached him and asked him to authenticate a painting. It was *La Femme à la Tête de Rose*. Dali was excited to see the picture, which he had lost track of. His affection for the painting was so overwhelming that he asked the man if he could buy it back. With a show of great reluctance, the smuggler finally agreed. Dali wrote a check, and the unknown man departed—doubtless laughing over the profits to be made from illicit art when a stolen picture could be so easily offloaded on the very man who had painted it.

Above: the scene after the theft of two precious crosses and a painting of the Madonna and Child by Pintoricchio. There are numerous unguarded churches in Italy with masterpieces worth a fortune to an unscrupulous dealer who is prepared to ask no questions, and the mechanics of breaking in require no sophistication.

Right: Pepe, one of the many mountaineer smugglers, with a pack on his back that can hold 15,000 cigarettes for a journey across the mountainous Swiss-Italian border country.

Far right: American cigarettes landed in Italy by a rubber dinghy, the perfect lightweight inflatable smuggling ferry.

Luxury Contra band 7

In the little Indian village of Murud on the shore of the Arabian Sea 150 miles or so south of Bombay, one day or one year is very much like all the others. The village life, with its never-ending rhythm of the farming community, runs from the present into the future with little to break the peaceful monotony. That's why the day that a small twin-engine plane came skimming in over the sea from the west soon after dawn, and touched down on the firm yellow sand of the beach, was a red letter day—a day to be talked about with excited wonder for months to come.

Men, women, and children poured out of their huts and ran toward the taxiing plane. Suddenly it lurched on a soft patch of sand and tilted forward, breaking the nosewheel and bending the propellors. Two men, looking both embarrassed and upset, scrambled out, pulling with them a pair of bulky suitcases. The pilot, a tall good-looking American, was traveling on a false British passport under the name of Peter Philby. He sought out the village headman from the crowd surrounding the up-ended plane, and asked his assistance. They had been forced to land because of engine trouble, he explained, and he and his copilot would have to go to Bombay in search of a mechanic to repair the

plane. Would the headman be so good as to mount a guard on the
plane until they returned with a mechanic? The headman was
honored to oblige his unexpected guests. If they wanted to get to
Bombay, he added, they could catch the bus up the road in a
little while. After paying generously in advance for a few hours
of guard duty, the two men set off. They had to drag the two
heavy suitcases behind them.

A few hours later the suitcases and contents had been safely
delivered to their destination in Bombay. Inside were nearly
1000 Swiss watches worth over $30,000 on the black market.

Although the delivery had been accomplished with only a
slight hitch, the problem remained of getting out of India before
the headman of Murud became suspicious about the two Englishmen. After all, they had been gone longer than it took merely to
get a mechanic. But Peter Philby and his companion were old
hands at difficult departures. The two men took a taxi to Bombay's Santa Cruz airport and, without being challenged, strolled
casually around the outside of the terminal building. They managed to mix with the passengers arriving on an East African
flight from Nairobi, go through immigration with them, and in

this way enter India legally. Then without further delay they took the first available seats on a flight out of the country—they didn't care where—before the headman back in the village thought of making inquiries about the two gentlemen and their plane. Since the plane had been hired under other false names, its loss was not a matter of concern to the smugglers.

The Watch Trade

For Peter Philby it was just another trick in a long smuggling career, a career that would continue for two more years until he was caught in Bombay with a haul of watches and diamonds. To him and countless others, the appeal of smuggling watches was simple: an easy way to make a great deal of money. For millions of Indians, a smart wrist watch is a status symbol; but the Indian government strictly limits the number of watches that can be imported, and places an exceedingly high duty on those that come in legally. A watch that can be bought in Hong Kong or Switzerland for a few dollars can be sold for four or five times as much on the Indian black market. In contrast to diamonds or gold, which can only be bought by the wealthy, a watch is something that most people need and can afford. India, with 575 million people, absorbs just as many wrist watches as the smugglers can supply. Upward of five million watches, worth about $200 million on the black market, are snuck into India every year.

Watches are smuggled by airline stewards and sailors who carry them in their overnight baggage or in specially made vests, something like those used for smuggling gold bars. The bulk of smuggled timepieces, however, flow along that already familiar pipeline from Dubai to Bombay aboard the custom-built smuggling dhows, often on the same boat with a shipment of 10-tola gold bars. Many of Dubai's merchants in fact find watches to be much more profitable than gold. Quietly sipping a soft drink as the air conditioner in his office whirrs behind him, a Dubai smuggling chief explains, "I know I can make $2 on every watch I send to India, but with gold nowadays the price fluctuates so much that it may be worth less when it arrives than when I sent it."

The Dubai merchants believe in delivering the illegal watches with professional skill. Each is wrapped individually in a thin plastic sheet and then in batches of 50 carefully slotted into strips of heavy plastic. Finally, 5000 watches are packed layer on layer in empty oil drums. When the tops of the drums are welded shut the watches are ready for the 1200 mile voyage to India. Even if the drums have to be thrown overboard and abandoned in shallow waters in an emergency, the watches will remain unharmed for a few weeks beneath the waves until they can be recovered by the smugglers.

The traffic pays so well that Dubai has become the third biggest buyer of Swiss watches after the United States and Britain. Dubai merchants import up to three million watches from Switzerland every year, along with another million or two from Hong Kong. Glancing at Swiss export figures and Dubai import figures, it looks as if each man, woman, and child in the little seaport buys about 50 watches a year. A handful of other tiny countries around the world also appear to have an insatiable addiction to watches. Kuwait buys about a million a year. Most of them are whisked over the desert to Iran. Panama is another big buyer, because seamen on ships going through the Panama Canal purchase dozens at a time to sell at a good profit throughout South America. The people of Libya seem to have the same extravagant taste, but the watches they import are destined for Egypt or, borne by camel across the Sahara, for Chad or Niger.

Much professional watch smuggling, however, is carried on within the watch trade itself as a profitable adjunct to legal dealing. Many dealers simply find it convenient to buy part of their supplies legally and part illegally. The art of the game is to make sure that the smuggled watches are exactly the same make as those imported openly. Because cheap watches are not numbered, the only precaution necessary is to make sure that the quantity of smuggled watches is the same or less than the quantity of legally imported ones. A dealer who passes 20,000 watches through customs legally must never be caught with more than 20,000 in stock.

Among American watch wholesalers there are a number who over the years have become adroit in these tactics. They buy 50,000 watches legally and another 20,000 illegally. They pay duties and taxes on the sale of the 50,000, but not on the 20,000 illicit watches. The whole traffic is so well organized that half a dozen Swiss manufacturers operated for years almost entirely for the smuggling trade. They would send an official consignment at the same time as an unofficial consignment that was going to its destination by the back door. The back door to the United States is usually that smuggler's paradise, the Mexican border town of Tijuana. One leading watch wholesaler there conveniently happened to have a cousin working for a Swiss firm making the cheap watch movements favored for smuggling. (The cases are made in the United States). A New York dealer wanting 30,000 watch movements would send a direct order for 20,000 to the Swiss firm, and another for 10,000 to a smuggler in Tijuana. Delivery from both sources was prompt. The Tijuana dealer usually sent the movements across the border in the roof of a car.

Not everyone got away with it, of course. In the most celebrated American watch smuggling case, the Valiant Watch Company in New York broke the rule that legal and illegal watches must always be of the identical make. The four brothers who ran Valiant had been bringing in all kinds of watches without carefully checking on the makes. After a time the United States customs authorities caught a couple of their couriers coming in from South America with 7000 watch movements. From the tale they told, customs was able to pinpoint the Valiant offices as the likely destination. On a surprise raid one day, they found 8000 watch movements that the four brothers could not account for in their books. They also found hidden all over the office $100,000 in small denomination bills in paper bags. Three of the brothers and several of the staff were promptly arrested, but there was not enough evidence to hold the fourth, who was released. He dashed out of the building, jumped into his car, and took off at high speed. Customs agents were discreetly on his tail. He drove straight to the home of one of his brothers already under arrest, hurried in the front door, and emerged minutes later clutching a package. It contained another 1000 smuggled watch movements.

A variation on the theme of matching legal and illegal imports of watches is regularly practiced in South America. From time to time customs authorities have auctions of watches that have been confiscated from smugglers. A dealer goes to the auction and buys, say, 1000 watches. He now has a good stock acquired from an impeccable source—customs itself. From then on the dealer sells only the kind of watch he got in the customs auction—but he buys his supply illegally. If he is ever asked the source of his stock he can show the documents from the customs' auction. Even if a good deal of time has passed since the government sale, he can usually explain it away as a period of slow business. He is fairly safe as long as his total stock does not exceed the 1000 watches he originally bought from customs.

The hazard for both smuggler and customer of watches is that

Below: a prize packaged and placed on display at Dover Town Hall by customs agents of the British port—a gas tank, inside of which was a smaller tank with 2581 watches carefully and well concealed.

the goods may be fake. For every genuine Swiss watch sold, there is probably another made in the Soviet Union, Japan, or Hong Kong to be sold as the real thing. The legend "Swiss made" on the dial is unfortunately no guarantee of the place of origin. If watches turn out to be fakes, there is nothing to be done. It is some consolation perhaps that even official dealers can be taken in. For example, the Bombay agent of a leading Swiss manufacturer once bought a consignment of his firm's watches that had been confiscated from a smuggler by the customs. A few days later he came back to the customs office in a fury. The watches they had sold him were fakes. Customs explained that no guarantee of origin was issued in auctions of confiscated goods.

The main source of most fake Swiss watches is Hong Kong. There an enterprising group of dealers make something of a speciality of putting together watches with cheap movements imported from the Soviet and Japan, as well as Switzerland, and sending them all over the East as high quality Swiss watches. Most are smuggled. A Hong Kong watch dealer, sipping his whiskey in the Dragon Boat Bar of the Hong Kong Hilton, once admitted: "I can't make any legitimate business in the Philippines or Taiwan or Indonesia. If I tried to sell direct to wholesalers there I wouldn't sell a watch."

While the motive for smuggling in Hong Kong is always mercenary, the profits are occasionally put to good use. For many years a self-styled bishop, who ran a seamen's mission in Hong Kong, was alleged to get visiting seamen to smuggle watches for him. He himself also made frequent trips around Southeast Asia in the cause of his mission, taking along some watches in his briefcase. All the proceeds of his smuggling enterprise were promptly ploughed back into his charitable work.

Below: the coat of Georges Geoffrey, a French diplomat passing through London. While being questioned by customs, he suddenly collapsed under the weight of the 298 watches sewn into the coat lining.

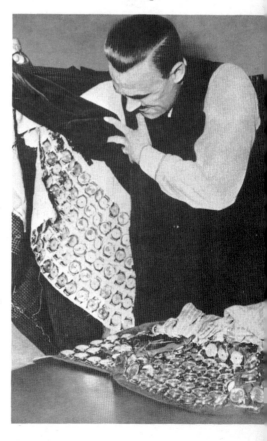

The Unexpected Response

Illicit operators hauling luxury goods like cigarettes and whiskey react to a chase by authorities in unpredicted ways. As a case in point, take the captain of a beat-up little Panamanian freighter, the 492-ton *Dany*. He was spotted by two French customs launches trying to slip into a remote harbor on the coast of Brittany with a contraband cargo of cigarettes and whiskey. When the launches tried to come alongside in heavy seas, the *Dany's* skipper put the helm hard over and headed for the open sea at full speed. The customs men opened fire with machine guns. Although the bullets clanged harmlessly off the *Dany's* hull, her captain began to fill the airwaves with distress signals claiming, "A warship has opened fire on my ship."

As the chase progressed, the *Dany's* skipper came on the radio again saying he would surrender only to a French naval vessel, as if he feared the customs launches might be pirates or a rival gang. The French navy actually ordered a destroyer to speed to the scene to head off the fleeing smuggler. By that time the chase had moved far outside French territorial waters, and the *Dany's*

Above: given an illegal cargo that will burn easily if customs officials appear to be closing in, more than one cigarette-smuggling captain has set fire to his ship. This one, called the *Omaca*, was pursued and seized off the Italian coastline—in spite of the heavy smokescreen.

skipper obviously felt he should be free from further interference. What he did not realize was that international law permits customs authorities to chase a smuggler outside their limits if they are in "hot pursuit." When the French destroyer came up, the *Dany* still refused to haul down her flag and surrender. Now about 60 miles at sea, the French vessels finally managed to maneuver alongside the Panamanian and put an armed boarding party aboard. Escorting their prize back to the port of Brest, the customs men blasted the *Dany's* captain with Gallic fervor and thoroughness. He had broken smuggling conventions by refusing to stop. "Normally cigarette smugglers play the game when they know they have been caught, and give themselves up without causing scenes," said a weary officer.

That officer was optimistic. He should have been thankful that the *Dany* did not fight back. Many of the rusty little freighters that ply the eastern shores of the Atlantic and the Mediterranean will illicit cargoes of cigarettes for such countries as Spain, Morocco, and Italy, are more than ready to do battle if they are caught. Italy's Guardia di Finanza (the police responsible for apprehending smugglers) tried to arrest the crew of another Panamanian cargo ship off Sicily only to have blazing Molotov cocktails tossed down as the official launches came alongside. They kept the Guardia men at bay during a six-hour chase while they tried to burn some of the 400 million contraband cigarettes aboard. In the end they only succeeded in making a bonfire of their ship, and had to take to the lifeboats.

Those 400 million cigarettes were a good haul, but small in relation to the 2.5 billion estimated to be smuggled into Italy each year—nearly 50 cigarettes for every man, woman, and child in the country. Some officials estimate that for every cigarette

Above: border guards of the Guardia di Finanza repair a hole in the Italian frontier fence on the border with Switzerland, which had been cut by cigarette smugglers. There are countless trails through the pine forests, and many wire clippers to cut fences.

Right: a customs officer, his automatic ready, challenges a suspicious character with a pack approaching him through the forest. For the officer there is always a discouraging possibility that the culprit, though one of a ring smuggling cigarettes, may not be carrying any of them himself. He could be the decoy to spring the trap.

legally bought in Italy, there are seven contraband ones. The reason for this wholesale flouting of the law is that the sale of tobacco in Italy is a government monopoly, and the cigarettes manufactured by the government-controlled factories hardly have the delicate aroma and flavorsome taste claimed by most cigarette advertisements.

Although American and other international brands are available at the government shops, they usually cost four times as much as the cigarettes purchased just over the border in Switzerland or from duty-free warehouses in half-a-dozen European ports. The smugglers make a fine profit by splitting the difference and charging about one-third less than the cigarettes available from the monopoly shops. They also offer almost as comprehensive a service as the government monopoly. It is safe to say that nearly every office and factory in Italy will be visited at least once a month by a traveling salesman with a suitcase full of contraband cigarettes.

Smuggling the Hard Way

Setting up a distribution network to rival the official monopoly calls for careful planning. Unlike gold, diamonds, or watches, a single smuggler can hardly carry a highly valuable cigarette consignment on his body or in his briefcase. Cigarettes must be moved by the ton, which is about one million cigarettes. The best ways are by ship or railroad freight. The only time that good old-fashioned muscle will suffice is on the short haul over the border from Switzerland into northern Italy. There the task is undertaken by gangs of *spalloni* (from the Italian word *spalla* meaning shoulder). On their broad shoulders these hardy mountaineers carry packs containing 15,000 cigarettes from Chiasso, Switzerland to lonely farmhouses just across the Italian frontier. Often they operate in groups of 30 or 40 at a time. On moonlit nights

Above: the lakes on the Swiss-Italian border are often busy in the comforting darkness of night. Here a Swiss customs boat stops two Italian smugglers, the Marcello brothers.

Right: in spite of the immense volume of smuggling, the Guardia di Finanza tots up some successes—often due to modern equipment like this helicopter and patrol vessel pursuing a motor boat used for smuggling.

Above: a customs agent frisks the Marcellos while another stands guard. The brothers specialized in ferrying gold, silver, narcotics, and currency across the mountain border.

Right: the brothers after their arrest. As with so many customs coups, the agents had had a tipoff by a helpful informer.

Above: one of the big problems with smuggling cigarettes is that they have to be moved in bulk to make a substantial profit. This photo of trucks with foreign cigarettes was taken from aboard a helicopter by the Guardia di Finanza at the mouth of the Oliva River.

they can be seen taking a carefully marked path over the hills through the pine forests to the border, where an accomplice will have cut a neat hole in the wire fence. The first two men in the contraband column carry empty packs as bait to spring any ambush. Once over the border, the spalloni dump their loads in the cellar of a safe house, and steal home through the night. Most boys on both sides of the border cut their teeth by smuggling cigarettes, and the local legend has it that no young lady will look at a man until he has made at least one trip. *Una consacrazione di virilita*, they call it.

The cigarettes will be picked up by truck and hurried to Milan, just half an hour down the highway. The main syndicates supplying all of Italy has its headquarters in Milan. The spalloni, however, can move only limited quantities of cigarettes. Most smugglers constantly try to work out plans to move them by the hundred thousands if not millions. Boats are ideal, especially for delivery to the Naples area or Sicily, and a veritable fleet of nondescript vessels plies the Mediterranean trying to satisfy the demand. An even better method is to distribute the cigarettes all over Italy by railroad freight, just like other consumer goods. That is precisely what happened a few years ago in a huge cigarette smuggling scandal that delighted all Italy.

The saga started when the prior of a poor Capuchin monastery in San Francesco just south of Rome was transferred to a monastery in Lugano, Switzerland. This just happens to be the town from which smugglers order most of their cigarettes. Within a few months of the prior's move, his former religionists in San Francesco suddenly began to show signs of prosperity. A couple of them even bought new cars. Clearly the monastery had some new benefactor. Indeed it had—a well-known cigarette smuggler. In talking to the new Capuchin prior in Lugano, the smuggler had realized that the monastery in San Francesco

would make a handy central depot from which to distribute his cigarettes to nearby Rome. After all, who would think of looking for contraband in a monastery? Could the kind prior arrange for the monks to help look after some goods for him? The prior agreed to oblige, and the smugglers arranged for a number of railroad freight cars to be loaded in Lugano with crates of "electrical equipment" destined for Israel via the Italian port of Genoa. They were coupled to a freight train and hauled into Italy. At the Milan depot, a suitably bribed railroad worker disconnected the cars from the Genoa train, changed their destination labels to read Rome-Capanelle, and saw them safely hooked onto a southbound train.

When the freight cars arrived at the rather lonely station near the Capanelle race track just outside Rome, the electrical equipment was unloaded by night onto a couple of trucks that sped away to the monastery of San Francesco. All went well for a time. Then one night when the smugglers were trying to maneuver a larger truck than usual through the monastery's narrow gateway, the vehicle got stuck. The driver panicked, revved up his engine, slammed into reverse gear, and backed out—pulling down the ornamental gates of the monastery and half the front wall. One smuggler, the supervisor, was killed by falling masonry, and another was badly injured.

The friars were distraught. One of them called the police to announce they had found a dead body they knew nothing about in their grounds. Another sped off with the injured man to a nearby hospital where he explained he had found the poor chap lying by the roadside, obviously the victim of a hit-and-run accident. When the police came, the monks changed their story. They tried to pass the whole thing off as an unfortunate result of their traditional Capuchin hospitality, saying that four travelers had asked for a night's lodging and had been welcomed in, fed,

Above: a truck loaded with timber artfully arranged to conceal a second load of smuggled foreign cigarettes.

Below: Father Antonio (center), a Capuchin monk whose transfer to Switzerland produced sudden remarkable wealth for his former monastery just south of Rome. It turned out that it had become a handy central depot for some cigarette smugglers.

and given a bed. In the middle of the night, the friars claimed, they had been awakened by the roaring of engines followed by screams. They had rushed out to find their front entrance demolished.

When the two casualties were found to be well-known smugglers, and abandoned crates found all over the monastery grounds proved to be full of cigarettes, the story fell apart. Just to compound it, a railroad employee at the Rome-Capanelle station, reading newspaper accounts of the escapade, noticed that the crates in the press photos were exactly like some still on three freight cars in the siding. Sure enough, they were also full of cigarettes. The prior and his friars were all convicted of aiding and abetting cigarette smuggling, despite the prior's plea in court that he thought he was helping some merchants store macaroni.

While cigarette smuggling into Italy often creates hilarity, the Guardia di Finanza, which is charged with the job of stopping it, takes the job with great seriousness. The guards like nothing better than a good cops-and-robbers style chase. They are under constant pressure to catch smugglers because the revenue from the government's cigarette monopoly accounts for almost 10 percent of Italy's income, and every puff on a contraband cigarette means less revenue for the government. The Guardia gets results. Operating with a highly integrated fleet of high-speed cars, motorbikes, and helicopters coordinated by a tele-printer network, the force seizes as many as 250 million cigarettes a year. Almost every day there is a picture in some Italian newspaper of proud Guardia di Finanza officers standing over a haul of a couple of tons of cigarettes. The only trouble is that while they are posing for the cameramen, one may be sure that another five tons are slipping in somewhere else. At least they are realistic about it. "Our coastline is 5000 miles long," said a Guardia di Finanza colonel. "We can't have men guarding every inch of it."

Smugglers who have problems with Italy's Guardia di Finanza can always divert their trade for a while to carrying whiskey to more friendly shores. Whiskey, like cigarettes, carries a high duty in most countries. All that is needed besides a reasonably seaworthy vessel are a few good connections.

When Tangier was a free port under international control, it was the center of the whiskey action. Scotch was shipped out of the free port on an armada of former motor torpedo boats manned by all kinds of adventurers. They received their delivery orders at sea from a high-powered shortwave radio operated by a leading Tangier merchant. Those carefree days came to an end when Tangier became part of Morocco. For a while Gibraltar, just across the sea, took over much of the business. A small coffee bar on the main street of the fortress town became the smugglers' hangout. One could sit there in the evening watching them make their plans for the next voyage. When Spain and Britain quarreled over Gibraltar's status in the late 1960s, Spain cut off all land, sea, and telephone communication with Gibraltar. Its usefulness as a smuggler's haven was severely curtailed. The whiskey smugglers then made Las Palmas in the Canary Islands their home base—with the result that the people of those Spanish islands suddenly seemed to acquire an unquenchable thirst for good Scotch. The islands now regularly import over 500,000 gallons of Scotch a year—enough for everyone living there to down 20 bottles. The Canary Islanders are not alcoholics of course. It is simply that the smugglers stock up on whiskey there and ship it to Spain, Morocco, and Algeria where legal whiskey is much more expensive. "This whiskey came from the Canaries," explained an English expatriate, pouring a generous libation in the living room of his Tangier home. "Officially whiskey here costs about 40 dirhams ($11) a bottle, but the booze coming in from the Canaries is only 22 dirhams. Can you blame me for buying it?"

The Whiskey Connection

Smugglers have their operation through the Straits of Gibraltar well organized. Their vessels show up regularly on the radar screens of British naval headquarters on Gibraltar, along with every other vessel passing into the Mediterranean, but no one worries about it too much. There is a story that one fleet of smuggling boats, operated by a fellow nicknamed El Canario, was so well known to Spanish and British patrol boats that they all exchanged salutes as they passed each other.

The citizens of a handful of small nations seem to be as exceptionally thirsty as the Canary Islanders. The people of the little West African state of Togo, for instance, appear to drink 25 times as much Scotch as their neighbors in Ghana. In fact the whiskey is being smuggled through the jungles from Lome, the Togo capital, into Ghana. Dubai, the smugglers' supermarket, naturally offers a dazzling array of Scotch among its wares. There is not much secret about what goes on. The annual review put out by The Scotch Whiskey Association is incidentally a handbook of who is smuggling how much. It lists in detail the amount of Scotch exported to every country—and those that are smuggling depots stand out. In addition to those already mentioned, Oman, Panama, Paraguay, Curaçao, and Malta all seem to have an excessive demand.

Much of the smuggling from such places is arranged informally by the captain and crew of passing freighters. For example, they will pool their resources as the ship goes through the Panama Canal, and buy up perhaps 50 cases of Scotch. They can be confident of selling these at a 100 percent profit in such South American ports as Lima or Valparaiso.

The whiskey makers themselves naturally keep quiet about the fact that some of their best customers are smugglers. Nonetheless they take pride in the fact that Scotch is the world's most smuggled alcoholic drink. As one manufacturer said rather disdainfully, "Did you ever hear of anyone smuggling gin?"

People, Parrots, and Pigs
8

The waters of the English Channel between England and France—the world's busiest shipping lane—are also among the most treacherous. From early spring to late autumn, scores of pleasure boats break down in the Channel; their crews are rescued by the lifeboatmen of Dover. A few seasons ago an emergency call to the Dover lifeboat station reported simply: "motor boat in distress four miles off the East Goodwin Sands." The lifeboat crew scrambled into their oilskins, and within five minutes were heading out of Dover into the choppy sea. For the lifeboatmen the rescue—like so many hundreds of others over the years—should have been routine. But they were in for a great surprise. When they maneuvered through clouds of spray alongside the drifting boat, a 30-foot motor launch named *Golden Sands*, they saw a line of frightened seasick faces peering through cabin portholes. And when they had towed the boat safely into Dover, they found a bevy of policemen waiting on the quay. Fourteen very shaky Asians, each clutching a small bundle of possessions, and the English pilot stepped ashore from the *Golden Sands*. They were all arrested.

The *Golden Sands* was no ordinary pleasure boat cruising innocently in the Channel. She was a key link in an organization that had been responsible for smuggling at least 500 illegal Asian immigrants into Britain. Three days before the incident in the English Channel a Belgian police informer, who had infiltrated the smuggler's ring in Ostend, had let it be known to the authorities that the *Golden Sands* was in port and her skipper busy lining up another illegal human cargo. The Belgians flashed an alert to the Illegal Immigration Unit of Scotland Yard, set up to counteract the multimillion dollar racket that smuggles upward of 5000 illegal immigrants into Britain every year—mostly from India, Pakistan, and Bangladesh. The Yard men had passed the word to the local police in Dover, and a trap had been set even before the *Golden Sands* pulled out of Ostend. In fact, it was a police helicopter shadowing the boat that had given the alert when she got into trouble.

There are tens of thousands of Asians living legally in Britain and thousands more waiting to come, lured by the prospects of better wages or by the desire to join family or friends already

Right: a secret compartment behind the back seat of a car modified for smuggling illegal immigrants into England by a German-based smuggling ring.

Below: a small army of illegal aliens brought across the border from Mexico to California, with the rented truck that carried them. The whole group, with the driver, was picked up by a border patrol at Chula Vista.

126

Above: a customs agent on the Kent coast in England, surveying one of the many shallow beaches on which it is all too easy to land a small craft without much chance of anybody noticing.

there. Because British immigration laws allow the legal entry of only a limited number each year, much immigration has been diverted into channels operated by the people smugglers.

Police believe that the captain of the *Golden Sands* was working for one of four main smuggling groups specializing in bringing Asians into Britain, and based in Belgium, France, the Netherlands, and West Germany. They provide a travel service that one policeman calls "as complete as Thomas Cook's." They arrange every minute of the journey from the time that the prospective immigrant leaves his home village on the Indian subcontinent until he is spirited ashore in Britain. For this service, the smugglers charge a minimum of $2000 per person. Estimates are that the annual profits are at least $10 million. The profits are so great, and the risks for the chief organizers who sit safely in Bombay or Karachi, Paris or Frankfurt, are so small that there is a cut-throat rivalry between the gangs for a good slice of what they call "body smuggling."

The immigrants, the unfortunate victims in the whole affair, pay at least 10 times the normal fare with no guarantee of safe arrival. Often they have to work for months in Britain to pay off their debt to the smuggling organizations. The initial leg of the journey to Belgium, the Netherlands or West Germany is usually no problem, because the British Commonwealth passport of the prospective immigrant allows free travel to every country but Britain. From then on, however, the journey is always tedious and often dangerous. Immigrants may have to wait four or five months in a strange unwelcoming city for a turn to be smuggled across the Channel.

When their turn comes to run the gauntlet, the hopeful immigrants may suddenly find themselves on a leaky boat or in a light plane in the dead of night. One smuggler even packed immigrants inside a freight container loaded with television sets for shipment across the Channel. Another racketeer stowed his

Right: a group of Pakistanis landing in England after they had been rescued from a rubber dinghy in which they had been found in the Channel. A German coaster saw their faint SOS signals made by flashlight. Below: the wet-suited smuggler who was accompanying them.

living cargo under the rubber flotation in the bilges of a speedboat being shipped back to Dover after a cross-Channel race. French customs officials, alerted one day by strange noises coming from inside a large tractor-trailer rig waiting to be loaded on a ferry, found 27 Asians stuffed like sardines in a five-foot-wide space under the trailer floor.

The April Diamond Scandal

When things go wrong, the Asians can expect little help from the smugglers as the case of the *April Diamond* showed all too clearly. The *April Diamond* was a battered 118-ton trawler owned by the British businessman John Rodger. Ostensibly it was supposed to carry supplies to oil and gas rigs in the North Sea. The supply runs provided perfect cover for illicit sidetrips to bring in illegal immigrants at $1000 a head. Rodger was the middleman between an Asian organizer known as "Charlie," based in the Netherlands, and operators in Birmingham. The Birmingham outfit supplied the transportation to pick up the immigrants as he put them ashore at night on lonely beaches on the east coast of England. When Rodger was ready to make a trip he would phone Charlie in Amsterdam, and agree on a rendezvous. Charlie would then round up his customers, usually from a rundown hotel in Amsterdam's redlight district, and take them by truck to some quiet Dutch port.

Above: John Rodger, the owner-skipper of *April Diamond*, after the Dutch authorities had closed in on the trawler during a smuggling run with 26 Asians aboard. He was arrested and returned to England, where he was convicted and imprisoned.

Charlie did not know that he was under surveillance by British and Dutch authorities who were preparing to spring a trap. So it was that late one night when he set out with 26 Asians for the fishing port of Scheveningen, the Dutch police alerted Scotland Yard. The Asians were stowed away on the *April Diamond*, which set sail across the North Sea toward England. During the voyage, however, word of the police operation leaked out to a journalist who tipped off a London evening newspaper and the British Broadcasting Corporation. Halfway across the North Sea, John Rodger—known to his friends not surprisingly as Jolly Rodger—suddenly heard on the radio that police were on the lookout for a trawler with illegal immigrants. He was in a dilemma. Should he go on or turn back?

Rodger decided to try to land the Asians as planned. As they neared the English coast he put a member of his crew, Ray Weber, over the side in a rubber dinghy with orders to paddle ashore to see if the coast was clear. The day was foggy and Weber, having seen that the beach was safe, could not find his way back to the *April Diamond*. Finally he was found drifting around, hopelessly lost, by the crew of a tug laying pipelines to a gas rig. They put him aboard the rig whose superintendent, having seen the news about the hunt for the trawler on TV, was at once suspicious. Weber was run ashore to the police.

Meanwhile, because Weber had not returned, Rodger dared

not take the *April Diamond* to the rendezvous beach. He turned and headed back to Scheveningen, slipping quietly into the little port in the early hours of the following morning. Just as he was about to tie up, the harbor was suddenly bathed in the glare of spotlights. The Dutch police were waiting in ambush. The *April Diamond* tried to make a run for it. Rodger and his crew could be seen urging the human cargo over the side into life rafts, and could be heard yelling at them "out . . . out." Some claimed later that they were thrown overboard and left to flounder in the water. Police commandeered a tug to block the harbor entrance and prevent the *April Diamond*'s escape. Rodger and his crew were arrested. Later, back in Britain, they were sent to prison for conspiracy to smuggle. As for the ditched Asians, they were all put on planes back to India and Pakistan. Because most of them were destitute, the Dutch government had to foot the bill.

The *April Diamond* case was cracked through good liaison between the British and Dutch police, but British detectives have also undertaken their own undercover inquiries in Europe. Detective Chief Superintendent Kenneth Clark of the Southwest Regional Crime Squad made six undercover trips to Paris without the knowledge of French police to penetrate a smuggling ring that had been smuggling Asians out of Cherbourg aboard a small ship, the *Marica*. Knowing that the *Marica* was suspect, her skipper and crew had holed up in France. Clark easily got in touch with the smugglers in Paris, telling them he was a writer who had come over to sell TV crime scripts to French television. Over a drink he also mentioned casually that he held a pilot's license. Maybe he could help fly a few immigrants to Britain in his private plane? At first the smuggler was suspicious, but Superintendent Clark stuck to his story about being a TV writer. He even went to the headquarters of French television to wander around inside when he thought he was being followed. Having convinced the smugglers that he was not a cop, Clark was introduced around. He finally located the skipper of the smuggling ship *Marica* hanging out in a British pub on the Champs Elysées. He tried to persuade him to return home, but the captain preferred exile to prison.

Clark also got a tip that two of the *Marica*'s crew were trying to slip back to London. He trailed them to the airport, watched them buy British Airways tickets, and phoned his men in England to meet all of that airline's flights from Paris. The trap nearly failed because at the last minute the men switched from British Airways to Air France. Clark saw what had happened, but could not tell his officers at London Airport because all lines to London were busy. Luckily the Air France plane was stacked outside London Airport because of landing delays, and Clark managed to get his call through as it touched down. The officers sprinted to the correct terminal, and arrived panting in the customs hall just as the wanted men came through.

Their arrest left the big organizers safe and unscathed in Paris. Within the framework of French law, they were doing

Above: illegal Indian immigrants on their way to a return flight to New Delhi, the end of their hopeful attempt to start a new life in Britain. They were picked up in England after having crossed the Channel in one of the many illegal boats.

The Kahlon brothers with one of the drivers of their smuggling ring.

The People Smugglers

There are many ways of getting people surreptitiously across the English Channel in order to evade immigration controls. One simple, but apparently very successful, method has been used by a smuggling ring reportedly in existence for 14 years. It takes Indians into England one at a time, but it has been estimated that the ring smuggles 5000 immigrants into Great Britain over a year.

The system was revealed to British journalists by one of the German drivers. The organizers are Indian brothers. The younger of the two brothers, Kuhlwand Singh Kahlon, lived in Bonn with his Scottish wife and three children. He had formerly worked for the Indian Embassy in Bonn, and had many influential contacts in that city. He had also once been a military advisor to the United nations in Israel. His older brother Sukwand feeds him customers through a travel agency in the town of Jullundur in the Punjabi district of India. The prospective immigrants are flown to one of several European capitals first, the favorites being Amsterdam, Copenhagen, and Brussels. Then they are transported by car to Cologne, where they stay hidden for four to five days while final arrangements are made.

The customers either have to pay approximately $10,000 each, or guarantee to pay it over 10 years to a sponsor in Britain. This covers the ferry trip, a passport, and about $3000 for the sponsor.

The other half of the arrangement is a modified car. A hidden compartment is built into the back seat, where the immigrant can be concealed during the cross-Channel trip and through the British immigration and customs checks. Each car is resprayed in a different color each week, and the license plates are regularly changed to avoid attracting undue attention. To prevent suspicion at the British ports where its cars arrive and depart within a matter of hours, the network used Indian observers to plot the regular pattern of duty hours, so that the drivers would only return after a duty shift. Sometimes the drivers brought their wives along for a bit of shopping while they were in England.

They had enough money to buy a good many things. Each trip made up to $800 for the driver, which he was paid in English pound notes. One driver claimed that he earned nearly $50,000 in one year.

Kahlon had a team of 30 drivers who picked up the immigrants from apartments in Cologne, took them across the Channel, and delivered them to specific addresses. The driver was then paid, and returned to Germany for another passenger. One man and his brother-in-law made a total of 134 trips to England in the four-month period between August and Christmas.

The simple secret of the ring's success lies in the immense number of cars—most of them, of course, perfectly legitimate — pouring through English ports from the continent. More than a million cars pass through the English channel ports each year, and any kind of a detailed check on individual cars would create an unacceptable delay for everyone. The result is that immigration men rely on spot checks, hunch, and experience.

To British reporters doing a story, Kahlon boasted that no one could touch him in Bonn, where he was not breaking any German law. But the reporters told Scotland Yard what they had learned from Kahlon—including details of routes and addresses in Great Britain at which immigrants had been and were dropped. When an investigation was started later, Kahlon's apartment was suddenly empty. The houses in Britain which had taken the newly arrived Indians from the German drivers were also vacant. Neighbors had no idea where the vanished occupants had gone so suddenly.

One top Scotland Yard detective said at the time that the reporters' story appeared in an English newspaper: "Immigrant smuggling is the wealthiest and fastest-growing criminal industry there is. And it's the most difficult to break."

So, as long as there is big money to be made in human cargo, the trade is likely to continue. As one driver said: "Kahlon has only to drive 60 miles to Belgium and continue the smuggling from there."

Left: the car leaves Cologne at dawn with an Indian passenger. Above: before they reach the port of Ostend, the passenger gets out and climbs into a secret compartment behind the back seat.

Above: there is just enough space in the compartment for the would-be immigrant to curl up, trying not to sneeze, cough, or make any noise whatsoever.

Right: the car drives onto the Dover ferry at Ostend, with apparently only one man in it.

nothing wrong, and could continue to rake in their profits. At the trial of the two men he had trapped, Superintendent Clark said he estimated that the syndicates he had identified in Paris were probably smuggling 2000 Asians into Britain each year.

The Mexican Traffic

While the cross-Channel body smuggling is certainly smuggling on a grand scale, it can hardly match the tidal wave of several million Mexicans illegally crossing the border into the United States each year. Compared to the 4000-mile haul of the Asians traveling to Britain, the flow of Mexican wetbacks (originally named that because they used to swim across the Rio Grande to get into Texas) is simply a mass commuter traffic. In a single recent year the Border Patrol of the United States Immigration and Naturalization Service turned back over 700,000 Mexicans trying to gain illegal entry, and arrested over 8000 smugglers of aliens. With its small force of less than 1500 men, the Border Patrol finds it almost impossible to police the whole 2000 miles of border between Mexico and the United States. One has only to sit in their checkpoint at Chula Vista, California, any night after dark to realize what they are up against.

Along some 80 miles of fence on either side of the checkpoint hundreds of electronic sensors have been planted in the ground to pick up the padding feet of the wetbacks as they come over.

Below: a United States border patrol agent implanting one of the automatic electronic sensor units used to detect movement near the border with Mexico.

Long before midnight, the telltale control panel is sparking like some firework display, and patrolmen go rushing out into the dark to intercept the hopeful border violators. They often travel in groups of 100 or more, led by professional smugglers. The patrolmen bounce the aliens back over the fence—and half an hour later they try again a few hundred yards away. Sometimes a single persistent man gets caught and sent back half a dozen times a night. By dawn perhaps 3000 people will have slipped through.

Originally the illegal entry into the United States by poverty stricken Mexicans in search of jobs was a matter of individual initiative. But today a border patrol officer notes that "organized smuggling rings have largely displaced the small-scale operations of former years. The smuggling of aliens into the country has become an extremely lucrative illegal venture." One ring known as *Las Hueras* (The Blondes), so named because it was run by three attractive women, is estimated to have made $9 million smuggling 36,000 Mexicans before being caught. One of the blondes lined up likely prospects in Tijuana, offering them counterfeit entry documents for a fee of about $200. Those who could not afford the price were given the alternative of carrying in a package of heroin or marijuana. They were then guided through the checkpoint at San Ysidro, California, and taken to a safe house in San Diego. The entry documents were collected and sent back to Mexico for reuse, while the illegal immigrants

Left: the printout from the sensor panel picking up signals from the units along the border, in a station in Del Rio, Texas.

Right: border patrol officers with a suspected illegal alien checking with headquarters for verification of his status.

were offered jobs on the big fruit fields nearby in California.

Another outfit dubbed "the Crystal City Four" operated out of Crystal City, Texas, and from a hotel in Piedras Negras just across the way in Mexico. Local Mexican agents signed up immigrants for a fee of anything up to $300, and put them up at the hotel as a staging post. At night they would cross the border at lonely Eagle Pass. There a fleet of large covered trucks waited to take them to log cabins along the Nueces River near Crystal City. They were kept in this second staging area for three or four days while arrangements were made to haul them in trailers to Dallas or Chicago. Often as many as 100 Mexicans were packed into a trailer for the journey. One of the Crystal City Four would scout the road ahead in a car on the lookout for any border patrol ambushes.

Smugglers often go to considerable trouble to outwit the patrolmen. Early one morning, for instance, a border patrol crew stopped an oil tanker on a lonely road in New Mexico. The driver protested that he was just hauling a load of crude oil, and to prove it he opened a valve in the side of the tanks to let oil spill out. In spite of this, something about his manner did not satisfy the officers. They climbed on top of the tanker and peered inside the hatches. The front and rear compartments were actually full of oil. But hidden in the center compartment, which was still four inches deep in oil, were 22 Mexicans packed into a space six feet long and six feet wide. Each had paid $300 to be taken across the border to Chicago.

Perhaps it was some consolation to them that they were all still alive in that confined space. Other wetbacks have been less fortunate. One scorching summer day the police in San Antonio, Texas, were called to inspect a closed truck parked in the full sun. Faint cries were coming from it. They forced open the locked back door to find 47 Mexicans crammed in the broiling interior. One was dead, two more were dying, and 15 others had to have hospital treatment for heat prostration. Those who could speak explained that they had all forded the Rio Grande River at night, and had been picked up by an American in a truck who took $100 from each of them. He had driven into San Antonio, locked them in the truck, and vanished with the money.

Above: the draw of higher wages, however low they might be in terms of other United States workers' pay, continues to draw wetbacks by the truckload across the long sparsely manned border. What usually happens to the aliens themselves is to be sent back to Mexico. Often they try again a few days or weeks later.

Tranquilized Parrots

Strange noises issuing from vehicles coming across the border do not always indicate humans. An inquisitive inspector in Brownsville, Texas, heard feeble squawks when he put his ear to the door of a cadilac. He removed the door panels to find 44 parrots that had been tranquilized in an attempt to keep them quiet during the crossing. In numbers that approach an annual bird migration, parrots are smuggled in from Mexico to avoid the lengthy 12-week quarantine required if they are brought in legally. The quarantine is to determine whether the birds are free from psittacosis, a disease carried by parrots

and parakeets and transmittable to humans. It is always a serious illness and sometimes fatal. A hungry parrot can munch a great deal of food during the quarantine period, so it is much cheaper and more profitable to disregard the quarantine and smuggle the birds in—particularly since a Mexican yellow-headed parrot that costs only $5 south of the border will bring $100 in an American pet shop. The only hazard is to keep the parrots from chattering noisily as they are sneaked past the customs post. The simplest solution is to get them drunk on tequila, although potential parrot smugglers should be warned that when the birds sober up they may be in for trouble. A parrot with a hangover is a most unsociable bird.

Smugglers show little concern for the welfare of the parrots. Customs officers once found 832 live parrots crammed into a tiny compartment specially built to house them beneath the floor of a Ford sedan.

The threat of prosecution seems to be no deterrent at all. One gang of parrot runners were caught in the United States and released on bail. They promptly embarked on another smuggling foray to pay for their lawyer's bill. The spirit of competition between rival gangs is expressed by frequent hijacking of birds from one another. Sometimes it is not just hijacking. One

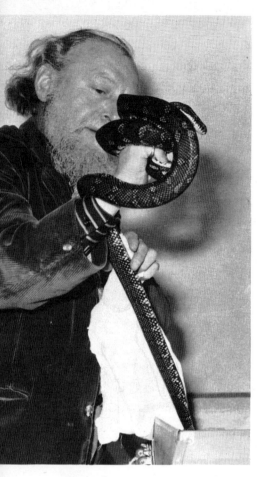

Above: a python rescued from the suitcase in which it came into Heathrow Airport, London. It was discovered with 14 other snakes after the suitcase was not claimed in the customs hall. The snakes went to London Zoo.

parrot runner not only had his birds stolen when his car was ambushed on a desert road, but also was left handcuffed to the steering wheel. He nearly died of thirst before being rescued.

Smuggling parrots is so profitable that the racket has become global. Australia is one of the prime sources of the birds. Many of the rarer ones bring high prices. A pair of Northern Rosellas, for example, is worth $4000 on the black market in Europe, while the brilliantly plumed Golden Shoulders or Superb Rosellas may sell at $8000 each. Even the pink and gray Galah, a parrot that many Australian farmers shoot as a pest, can command $150 in Amsterdam.

Parrots are smuggled out of Australia on commercial jets, either in falsely labeled freight containers or as baggage. Some are flown on private aircraft to Indonesia. They are doped to keep them quiet with the drug Luminal, which is injected into their breasts. Many do not survive the treatment, but the profit margin is so high that even if only one bird in 10 survives the journey, the smuggler is still ahead of the game. The racket is so lucrative that the director of a special 20-man squad set up by the Australian Federal Customs Department to combat it believes that many Australian professional criminals are now giving up the dangerous life of bank robbery and other violent crime in favor of an easier life running parrots.

$1000 for a Smuggled Snake

Smuggling rings are now known to be branching out to trade in other rare Australian animals, especially reptiles. For instance, Taipan snakes, an aggressive and lethal species found in northern Australia, are in big demand by owners of American snake farms. They are willing to pay up to $1000 for a single specimen. Shipping them out illegally apparently presents no problem. "The risks are minimal," explains an agent of the Australian National Parks and Wildlife Service that is trying to stop the traffic. "Snakes can be wrapped in a parcel and mailed at any post office. They can go for weeks without any food or water and, above all, they do not squeak.

The growing determination of many countries to save their endangered wildlife has created a growth market for smugglers prepared to dodge the new regulations in order to supply unscrupulous private zoos. The orang-utan, which is in danger of extinction in its native home of Borneo and Sumatra, can command well over $2000 on the animal black markets of Europe or the United States. There are less than 5000 of these apes left in the wild, and their export from Borneo and Sumatra is officially forbidden. Although customs in neighboring Singapore and Thailand have been alerted to watch out for these animals in illegal transit, the traffic is hard to stamp out. Sailors may pick up a baby orang-utan from a Bornese or Sumatran dealer who has shot the mother. They will keep it with them until they can slip it ashore secretly and sell to a dealer. This dealer in turn may

forward the baby ape to his client as part of a large batch of monkeys, trusting that customs men will not look at the shipment closely enough to realize that it contains an orang-utan.

The real job of stopping the racket is usually left to enthusiastic wildlife conservationists like Tom Harrisson, the former curator of the Kuching Museum in Malaysia. He has tirelessly tracked down illicit animal dealers all over Southeast Asia. Often he bluffs his way in to see their collections, posing either as a tourist or a potential buyer. On spotting an orang-utan or other rare wildlife whose movement is controlled, he reports it to the International Union for the Conservation of Nature, which makes a protest to the government concerned.

This hide-and-seek war with international smugglers has no limits. People, parrots, and rare birds and animals are merely a part of it. The Irish run pigs from Ulster into Eire, and West Africans run cattle by the thousand from Niger into Nigeria. The smuggler's catalog, in fact, includes anything that is prohibited or limited in legal trade.

For many years there was a flourishing trade in smuggling human hair for wigs into the United States. The traffic developed because, until the mid-1970s, the United States prohibited the importation of anything from Communist China, and China is one of the best sources of the long black tresses that

Above: a dead puma found in a packing case in London. Animals are often shipped in appalling conditions, and the necessary secrecy of the smuggling trade prevents their rescue in time.

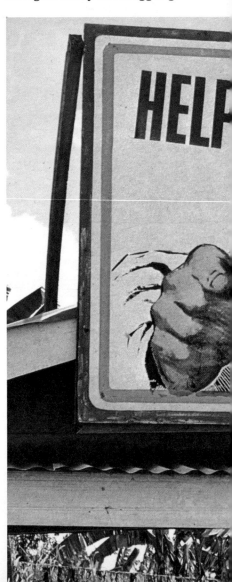

wig makers require. To get around the regulation, hair was sent into the United States with false certificates of origin, claiming it was from Hong Kong. After a time it became clear that if all the imported hair was coming from Hong Kong, every female in the British Crown Colony must be bald. Hong Kong certificates were no longer accepted. The result was the game of "swimming hair." The tresses were still shorn from Chinese heads, but "swam" to Indonesia, Malaysia, or even Portugal, where many women also have long black hair. It was then rerouted to the United States with certificates of origin from those countries. A variation on the theme was to claim that the hair came from yaks, but customs laboratories soon detected otherwise. Hair smuggling declined after the United States reestablished relations with China. But the game still goes on with tresses from North Korea, whose goods are still prohibited.

In many developing countries the smuggler may help to overcome shortages of basic necessities. Vitamins are smuggled into India, and everything from car tires—worth $200 each—to medicine and nuts and bolts find their way into Burma. Some feel that the Burmese economy might collapse entirely without the black market lifeline through Thailand that keeps people supplied with many essentials denied them by an isolationist government. In Burma and in other developing nations the black market is almost like the corner grocery store elsewhere. At a dinner party in Manila, for example, a Filipino hostess may serve an exotic local dish garnished with a richly spiced meat sauce. If a guest asks for the recipe, she will have to admit that the crucial spices are to be had only from smugglers—although that creates little problem. In fact, smuggling has long been so rampant in the Philippines that a few years ago the president embarked on a nationwide antismuggling campaign. Huge billboards along the roadsides proclaimed: "Help Stop Smuggling and Make This Nation Great Again." The appeal brought little response from the smugglers or their eager clients.

Perhaps the clue to all the world's smuggling can be found by reading the great Russian writer Dostoyevsky. In his book *The House of the Dead*, he gives one of the best insights into the smuggler's mind. "A smuggler," he wrote, "works from inclination, from passion. He is on one side an artist. He risks everything, runs terrible dangers; he is cunning, invents dodges, and gets out of scrapes, and sometimes acts with a sort of inspiration. It is a passion as strong as gambling."

Index

Caption references are shown in italics

ADPRIN, Automated Data Processing Intelligence Network, 19
Afyon province, Turkey, 24, 37, *37*
Algeçiras, Spain, 50, 56
Algeria, *47*, 51, 52, 53
Amsterdam, 44, 58, *58*, 129, 138
animals, smuggling of, 136-9, *140*
antiques, smuggling of, 8, 18, 94-110
Antwerp, 10, 59, 87, 90
Archaeology, British Institute of, 94, 97
Art and Antiques Squad, 110
Art and Antiques Weekly, 110
art treasures, smuggling of, *4*, 8, 18, 94-111; theft of, *94*, 100-1, 102, 107-8, *111*
Asunçion, Paraguay, 24, 27
auctions, by customs authorities, 116, 117
Australia, 138; Federal Customs Department of, 138; National Parks and Wildlife Service of, 138
authentication, of art works, 94, 107, 111
Aztec treasures, *106*

baffles, fiberglass, 59
Bangkok, 28, 39, 40, 43, 71, 76, 93
Bangladesh, 100, 126
Beirut, 10, 58, 68, 69, 71
Belgium, 77, 111, 126
Bianchi, Cesar Medice, drug smuggler, 22-5, *22*
boa constrictors, 16
boats, smuggling by, 35, 60, *120*, 122, 126-31; *see also*, dhows
"body smuggling," 128
Bombay, 72, 112-4
bookkeeping, "creative," 17
Boston Museum of Fine Arts, 103-4, *104*
Boucan, Captain Marcel, French smuggler, 35, *36*
Brazil, 66, 93
bribery, 73, 81-2
Britain, 71, 126-8
Bromley, Catherine Anne, Welsh smuggler, *73*
Brussels, 10, 58, 68
Burma, *4*, 37, 140; Shan States of, 28, 43

Calmet, Georges, French drug chemist, 30, *30*, *32*
camel caravans, 67
cannabis, 10, 17, 21, 44-63; *see also* hashish, marijuana
Cannabis sativa, 44
Caprice des Temps, *34*, 35, *35*
cars, drugs smuggled in, 48-54, 56, 61; gold smuggled in, 68, 77; people

smuggled in, *126*
Casablanca, 49, 53
cattle, smuggling of, 139
charas, 44
chessboard, *61*
chewing gun, 86
children, as mules, *14*, 15
China, hair from, 139
Choi Tai Fook, gold dealer, 70
Chula Vista, California, *126*, 134
churches, *94*, 101, 110, *111*
cigarettes, *15*, *21*, 24, 35, *112*, 117-124, *123*
cocoa, 9
Cologne, Germany, 132
Commission for the Recovery of Works of Art, 103
commune, "Let it Be," 56, *56*
computers, 6, *19*, 20
Consolidated Diamond Mines, 85
contraceptives, 82, 93
Copenhagen, 44, 58
copies, of paintings, 111
Corsicans, 29-30
Croce, Jean-Baptiste, Corsican heroin smuggler, 36, *36*
Curaçao, 71, 125
currency smuggling, 11, *14*
customs agents, 15-6, *17*, *18*, *21*, *61*, 117, *128*
customs declarations, false, 92

Daily Mirror, 111
Dali, Salvador, 111
Davey, Timothy, British boy drug smuggler, *54*
De Beers, Central Selling Organization, *84*, 87, *88*
Delgado, Joseph, British hashish smuggler, *48*
dhows, *9*, 65, *66*, 72, *75*
Diamond Detective Division, S. African police, 86
Diamond Mining Company, Sierre Leone, 80, *83*
diamonds, 8, 10, 79-94
diplomats, smuggling by, 12-5, *117*
dogs, *53*, 63
Dorak, Royal Treasure of, 94-99, *96*
Dover, England, *116*, 126
Drug Enforcement Agency, 18, 20
drug smuggling, *17*, 28, 39, *54*; routes, 28; *see also*, cannabis, hashish, heroin, marijuana
Dubai, 10, 68, 71, 72, 125; gold smuggled from, *9*, 65-6, *66*, *75*; watches smuggled from, 114-5

Eagle, car ferry, 48
Egypt, 66, 101
Ekholm, Dr. Gordon, Mayan expert, 107
elderly people, as mules, 15-6, 54
Etruscan tombs, *100*, 102-3, *102*, *103*
Euphronios, Greek painter, *100*, 101
Euxithos, Greek potter, 101

family groups, as smugglers, 54
Femme à la Tête de Rose, La, 111
fish sauce, 76
Fleming, Ian, thriller writer, 82

food, smuggling of, 8
Foreign Trade Representations Inc., 37
Fowler, Howard, American hashish smuggler, *51*
France, 36, 66, 68, 77, 117, 128
Francis, Lynn, British girl currency smuggler, *14*
Frankfurt, 11, 88
freight trailers, 129, 136
French connection, 28-37

ganga, 44
Gazeezoglu, Kemalettin, Turkish governor, 37
Geneva, Switzerland, 8, 10, 68, 108
Geoffrey, Georges, French watch smuggler, *117*
Germany, West, 58, 77, 128
Ghana, 9, 87, 125
Gibraltar, 50, 124, 125
glass eye, in smuggling, 92
gold, bars, *6*, *66*, 68-9; smuggling of, 6, 8, 9, *9*, 10, 16, 65-77
"Golden Triangle," *4*, 37, *38*
Guardia di Finanza, 118, *119*, 122, *122*

hair, human, 139
Harris, Mike, American drug smuggler, *9*
hashish, 44, *46*, *51*, *53*, *58*, *59*, *60*, *61*
Hassan, King of Morocco, 44
Hatton, Roy, head of Hong Kong customs, *41*
Hecht, Robert E. Jr., American art dealer, 101, *101*
Hernandez-Noa, Luis, Cuban diamond smuggler, *92*
heroin, price of, 10; smuggling of, *4*, 8, 12, *13*, 16, *17*, 20, 22-43; brown, 37, 58
hijacking, *19*, 71, 137
Hong Kong, 10, 28, 39, 43, 68, 71, 93, 114, 115, 117, 140

IDB, illicit diamond buying, 82, 88
IDM, illicit diamond mining, 8, *80*, 86
IDSO, International Diamond Security Organization, 88, *89*
Illegal Immigration Unit, 18, 126
Illustrated London News, 97, *99*
India, 68, 72, 73, 89, *131*; gold smuggled into, 65, 67, 69, 72-5; watches smuggled into, 112-4
Indochina, Bank of, 75
Indonesia, 66, 69, 76, 138
informers, *121*
International Union for the Conservation of Nature, 139
Interpol, 20, 49, 89, 107, 110
Iran, 58, 65, 115
Italy, 66, 89, 101, 102, 110, 118-24
Izmir, Turkey, 94

jackets, smuggling, *6*, *66*, 70, 71, *73*
jails, *9*, *44*, *54*
Japan, 39, 67, *72*, 89, 90, 117
jewelry, 72, 92-3
Johnson Matthey, gold dealers, *69*, 70
junks, *40*

Kahlon Brothers, Kuhlwand and
    Sukwand, 132
Kennedy Airport, *27*, 59
Kenya, *14*, 15
Ketama, Morocco, 44, *47*, 56
kif, 44, *47*
Kim Tranh, gold bars, 70, 76
King Fook, gold dealer, 70
Koidu, Sierre Leone, 80-3
Kourlian, Kirkran, Jordanian gold
    smuggler, *72*

laboratories, drug, 30, *30*, *32*
Laredo, Texas, 6, *19*, *21*
Latin American Connection, 24-7
Laws, Teresa, British girl currency
    smuggler, *14*
Lebanon, *53*, 66
Liberia, 83
Lloyd, Professor Seton, 97
Locarno, Switzerland, 108
London, 10, 44, 66, 68, 77
"Lowland Weed Compagnie," *58*
LSD, 16
Luminal, 138

Mafia, 29, 89
Maggiore, Lake, Italy, *15*
mail, smuggling by, 90
Malaysia, 69, 139
Manilla, Phillipines, 93
Marcello brothers, Italian smugglers,
    120, *121*
Mari, Joseph, French drug smuggler,
    36, *36*
marijuana, *9*, 17, 44, 58, *63*; plant, *46*
Marro, Joseph, French drug smuggler,
    37
Marseilles, *17*, 19, 28-30, *30*, 51, 53
Martin, Mrs. Frances, 55
Maya art treasures, *107*; masks, 105,
    106
Mellaart, James, British archaeologist,
    94-9, *96*
Metropolitan Museum of Art, 101
Mexican immigrants, illegal, *126*, 134
Mexico, 6, 16, 58, 60-3, 72, 101;
    people smuggled from, *128*, 134-6;
    parrots smuggled from, 136-7
Meyer, Karl, author, 105
Miami, Florida, 22, 35, 93
Milan, Italy, 87, 122
Molotov cocktails, 118
Monastery, Capuchin, 122-4, *123*
Monrovia; Liberia, 83
Morocco, 44, *46*, *47*, 55-6, 57, 58, 66,
    68
morphine base, 30, *32*, *39*, *40*
Mounties, 15
mules, *6*, 10, 22-6, 34, 49, 70-1, 92
museums, 100, 101, 102, 103, *104*,
    139
Muslims, 46

nails, gold, 67
narcotic squads, *16*, *17*, 36, *40*, 53
Narcotics Preventative Service, Hong
    Kong, *41*
National Drugs Intelligence Unit, 49, 52
Natural History, American Museum of,

101
Netherlands, 58, *58*, 128
New York, 10, 32, 44, 87
New York Times, 101
Nixon, Richard M., 27

opium, *16*, *18*, 24, 37, *61*; poppy, *22*,
    29, *30*, 37, *37*, 39; in Shan States,
    43
Oppenheimer, Sir Ernest, chairman of
    De Beers, 88
orang-utan, 138
Oriental Connection, 28, 37-43
oscilloscopes, 32
Ovambo tribesmen, 85

Pakistan, *57*, 65, 69
Panama, 115, 125; Canal Zone, 26
Papastrati, Anna, 94, *99*
Paraguay, 24, 28, 35, 125
Pardo-Bolland, Salvador, Mexican
    Ambassador, *12*, 14, 15
Paris, 87, 131; Bourse, 77
parrots, smuggling of, 8, 136-8
Parthenon, Athens, 101
passports, 50
Pelikanstraat, Antwerp, 90, *90*
people, smuggling of, 19, 126-36
perfume, 18, 30
Phillipines, 92, 141
Piero della Francesca, 108
pigs, smuggling of, 139
Pintoricchio, Italian painter, *111*
planes, private, in smuggling, 86, 112,
    131, 138
plates, *60*
Plundered Past, The, 105
pop groups, 59
pot, 44, *44*
pre-Columbian art, 105, 107
Pritchard, Detective Constable Martin,
    57
psittacosis, 136
puma, *139*
python, *138*

quarantine, 136

Raphael, Italian painter, 103, *104*, 108
Reading, England, 56, *56*
Ricord, Auguste Joseph, Corsican drug
    smuggler, 24, *25*, *27*, 34
Rif district, Morocco, 44, 46
Rio Grande, Texas, 6, 134
rocket, homemade, 85
Rodger, John, British businessman,
    129, *130*

Saenz, Dr. Josue, Mexican collector,
    105
Saigon, 40, 75
San Ysidro checkpoint, 61, 135
Scotch Whisky Association, 125
Scotland Yard, 18, 49, 56
Shan States, 28, 43
shaving cream, 92
Shiva, bronze statue of, *107*
shoes, 17; heels of, in smuggling, 92,
    92
Sierre Leone, 8, 80-5

Sillitoe, Sir Percy, 88, *88*, *90*
silver, 65, *67*, 72
Simon, Norton, California collector,
    106, *107*
Singapore, 10, 28, 39, 66, 68, 69, 77,
    93
Siviero, Rodolfo, Italian detective, 103,
    105, 108
snakes, 16, 138, *139*
South Africa, 68, *68*, 77, 86
Soviet Union, 68, *68*, 88, 117
Spain, *9*, 44, *47*, 49, 68, 124
spalloni, 120
submarines, *15*
suitcases, *12*, 13, 15
Sureté Nationale, 51, 52
Switzerland, 66, 77, 114, 120

Taipan snakes, 138
Tangier, 44, 49, 124
teak logs, 17, *40*
TECS, Treasury Enforcement
    Communication System, *19*
teeth, smuggling in, *92*
tequila, 137
Thailand, 37, 66, 75, 93, 141
Tijuana, Mexico, 10, 61-2, 115, 135
Togo, 9, 125
tombaroli, 102, *102*
tombs, 102, *102*
Toorenaan, Chief Superintendent, *14*
toothpaste, 92
trailers, car, smuggling in, 48, *48*, *49*
training, of mules, 11, 70
Truckers Bible, The, 49, *50*, *51*
Turkey, 16, 37, *37*, *54*, 66, 68, 94

undercover agents, 21, 28, 41-3, 62, 86
United States, *54*, 66, 89, 90, 91;
    Bureau of Customs, 19, 21; Bureau
    of Narcotics and Dangerous Drugs,
    18, 26; Customs Agency Service,
    18; Immigration and Naturalization
    Service, 134; Treasure, Assistant
    secretary of, 104
Universal Studios, 63
Urbino, Ducal Palace of, 108

Valiant Watch Company, 115
Vasan, Albert, French drug chemist, 30,
    30, *32*
vases, Greek, *100*, 101, 103
Vientiane, Laos, 68, 75-6
Vietnam, South, 75, 76; war in and
    drugs, 28, 39, 75-6
vitamins, 140
Vorrink, Irene, Dutch Minister of
    Health, 58

watches, smuggling of, 8, 10, 17,
    113-8, *117*
Weitman, Leiser, diamond smuggler, *92*
wetbacks, 134, *136*
whiskey, smuggling of, 24, 124-5

X-ray machines, 19, *19*, 44, 85

Yao tribe, *38*

Zurich, Switzerland, 10, 67, 68, 102

143

Picture Credits

Key to picture positions : (T) top (C) center (B) bottom ; and in combinations, e.g. (TR) top right (BL) bottom left

2	Martin Patternotte/Camera Press	
4	Francisco Hidalgo/Colorific!	
7	John Perkins/*Daily Telegraph* Colour Library	
8	*Radio Times* Hulton Picture Library	
9(L)	John Perkins/*Daily Telegraph* Colour Library	
9(R)	Robert Royal/Camera Press	
12(TL)	U.P.I. Photo, New York	
12(TR)-13	Royal Canadian Mounted Police	
14(L)	Keystone	
14(R)	Michael Sheil/*Daily Telegraph* Colour Library	
15	Popperfoto	
16	Pierre Boulat ©Time Inc. 1976	
17(L)	Photo Jean Marcilly	
17(R)	Bob Peterson ©Time Inc. 1976	
18(B)	*Radio Times* Hulton Picture Library	
19(L)	By courtesy of Topix	
19(R)	U.S. Customs Service	
20	Bob Peterson ©Time Inc. 1976	
21(R)	Rolf D. Schurch/Camera Press	
22(L)	Ian Bodenham/Camera Press	
23	R. Azzi/*Daily Telegraph* Colour Library	
24-27	U.P.I. Photos, New York	
29(T)	Ann Dunn ©Aldus Books	
29(B)	R. Azzi/*Daily Telegraph* Colour Library	
31(T)	Photo Jean Marcilly	
31(B), 32	Michael Hardy/*Daily Telegraph* Colour Library	
33	*Daily Telegraph* Colour Library	
34(L)	Agence France Presse/Press Association	
35(T)	Michael Hardy/*Daily Telegraph* Colour Library	
35(B), 36	Agence France Presse/Press Association	
37	R. Azzi/*Daily Telegraph* Colour Library	

38	Alexander Low/*Daily Telegraph* Colour Library
39, 40(L)	Timothy Green
41	Martin Patternotte/Camera Press
42	Alexander Low/*Daily Telegraph* Colour Library
44	Co. Rentmeester ©Time Inc. 1976
45, 46(L)	Pierre Boulat ©Time Inc. 1976
46(R)	Robert Royal/Camera Press
47(R)	Pierre Boulat ©Time Inc. 1976
48-49	Photos by permission of H.M. Customs and Excise
50(L)	Photos Mark Edwards ©Aldus Books
51(L)	Pierre Boulat ©Time Inc. 1976
51(B)	Robert Royal/Camera Press
52	Dante/Camera Press
53, 54(L)	Pierre Boulat ©Time Inc. 1976
54(R)	U.P.I. Photo, London
55	Transworld
56(L)	Photo White & Reed ©Aldus Books
57	Photos by permission of H.M. Customs and Excise
58	Adam Woolfitt/Susan Griggs Agency
59	Michael Sheil/*Daily Telegraph* Colour Library
60-61	U.S. Customs Service
62-63	U.P.I. Photos, New York
64	John Perkins/*Daily Telegraph* Colour Library
66-67(T)	Timothy Green
67(B)	John Perkins/*Daily Telegraph* Colour Library
69(TL)	Terence Spencer/Colorific!
69(TR)	Timothy Green
69(B)	John Perkins/*Daily Telegraph* Colour Library
71	Timothy Green
73	Popperfoto
74	John Perkins/*Daily Telegraph* Colour Library
75	Popperfoto
78-86	James Pickerell/*Daily Telegraph* Colour Library
87(L)	De Beers Consolidated Mines, Limited

87(R)	Adam Woolfitt/Susan Griggs Agency
88	Popperfoto
89(T)	*Rand Daily Mail*
89(B)	De Beers Consolidated Mines, Limited
91	J. van der Hagen/*Daily Telegraph* Colour Library
92	U.P.I. Photo, New York
93(T)	Keystone
93(B)	U.S. Customs Service
95	Francisco Hidalgo/Colorific!
96-97	Kenneth and Patricia Pearson
98	*Illustrated London News*
99	Kenneth and Patricia Pearson
100	U.P.I. Photo, New York
101	Jean-Pierre Couderc/*l'Express*
102(T), 103(L)	Velio Cioni/Roma's Press Photo
103(R)	ANSA/Press Association
104-105(T)	U.P.I. Photos, New York
105(B)	Associated Press
106(T)	U.P.I. Photo, New York
106(B)	Bill Eppridge ©Time Inc. 1976
108, 109(T)	Palazzo Ducale, Urbino/Scala, Florence
109(B), 111	ANSA/Press Association
112	Rolf D. Schurch/Camera Press
113	Guardia di Finanza, Rome
116	Associated Press
117	Keystone
118	Guardia di Finanza, Rome
119(L)	Timothy Green
119(R), 120-1(T)	Rolf D. Schurch/Camera Press
121(B), 122-3(T)	Guardia di Finanza, Rome
123(B)	Associated Press
127(T)	*Stern Magazine*
127(B)	Official U.S. Border Photo, Chula Vista, California
128	Adam Woolfitt/*Daily Telegraph* Colour Library
129(TR)	Keystone
129(B), 130	Central Press
131	Keystone
132-133	*Stern Magazine*
134-137	Official U.S. Border Photos, Chula Vista, California
138-139	Aerpix Press
140(T)	Photo David Parker
141	Timothy Green

Both author and publisher wish to acknowledge their debt to *The Dorak Affair*, by Kenneth Pearson and Patricia Connor, published by Michael Joseph, 1967, for details of the Mellaart story told in Chapter 6.